Happy Birthday

Understand you are an excellent gardner — hope this will interest you and add to your knowledge

Love —

E
B
J
J
&
J

Plants Under Lights

JACK KRAMER

DRAWINGS BY ADRIÁN MARTÍNEZ

SIMON AND SCHUSTER · NEW YORK

COPYRIGHT © 1974 BY JACK KRAMER
ALL RIGHTS RESERVED
INCLUDING THE RIGHT OF REPRODUCTION
IN WHOLE OR IN PART IN ANY FORM
PUBLISHED BY SIMON AND SCHUSTER
ROCKEFELLER CENTER, 630 FIFTH AVENUE
NEW YORK, NEW YORK 10020

SBN 671-21688-0
LIBRARY OF CONGRESS CATALOG CARD NUMBER: 73-19097
DESIGNED BY EVE METZ
MANUFACTURED IN THE UNITED STATES OF AMERICA
PRINTED BY THE MURRAY PTG. CO., FORGE VILLAGE, MASS.
BOUND BY THE BOOK PRESS, NEW YORK, N.Y.

1   2   3   4   5   6   7   8   9   10

ACKNOWLEDGMENTS

It would be impossible to list names of all the people at various lighting companies who gave freely of their information and supplied literature and catalogs. Thus, let me thank all concerned at the companies listed below for their gracious help and for their enthusiasm for this book:

    Halo Lighting Company
    GTE Sylvania
    General Electric Company
    Westinghouse Electric Company
    Lights of Marin

    And special thanks to the Indoor Light Gardening Society of America.

I also would like to express gratitude to my editor, Julie Houston, whose enthusiasm and verve for this book matched mine.

Contents

CONTENTS

Introduction

Today, more than ever before, more people want living indoor plants as part of their surroundings. Plants do more than fill space; they give a feeling of well being and they add decorative accents. But in many cases—especially in apartments—natural light from windows is at a minimum or even nonexistent. Yet even in these situations, lovely indoor plants are possible because with artificial light plants will grow even in dim corners. An exciting new world of freedom for plants and plant lovers now exists.

With artificial light—fluorescent and incandescent—you don't have to worry about plants' suffering from lack of light on cloudy days. You control the "sunshine" with a flick of the switch, and you can grow plants almost anyplace in a room.

Because of their design, fluorescent tubes lend themselves to tray, shelf, bookcase or under-counter areas. In such places, small or medium-sized plants provide a lovely green accent—and fluorescent lamps in custom-made planters make it possible for you to have beautiful and thriving decorative green islands indoors away from windows. This book includes several handsome planter designs with step-by-step instructions for living-room situations.

Incandescent light, too, can be a plant saver. With floodlights you can maintain large, mature interior plants as a structural part of the room design. Incandescent lights in appropriate fixtures will keep them growing for years, while otherwise they might perish.

There are many books on artificial light gardening, but none include attractive planter designs and setups for rooms in the home. And few mention the benefits of incandescent lighting to maintain and display plants. This book introduces new ideas and concepts for growing plants under artificial light, whether on a small or a large scale.

Plants Under Lights can be used as supplemental reading to any other book about artificial light gardening; on its own it will provide new ways to utilize plants and light functionally and aesthetically.

JACK KRAMER

1·Seeing Plants in a New Light

THERE ARE MANY SOURCES of light, but fluorescent and incandescent light are primarily used for growing plants indoors, although mercury vapor lamps are occasionally used too. Fluorescent lamps are limited mainly to shelf gardening with small plants because the maximum distance they can be placed above plants is 18 inches, and also because of their tubular design. Exceptions are especially designed planters to accommodate fluorescent tubes that will allow the growing of larger plants to some extent.

Trays and carts are examples of self gardening; they are generally used in basements or attics for hobby gardens. Some have one shelf, others have two or three. You can buy commercial tray or cart units from suppliers, or you can make your own attractive setups in bookshelves, cupboards or whatever for room situations; just remember that with this kind of setup you can grow only small plants.

Incandescent lamps (the ones we read by) accent plants and help them grow. In handsome bullet-shaped or canopy fixtures, incandescent floodlamps allow you to decorate with plants in room corners far from windows, and floodlamps of

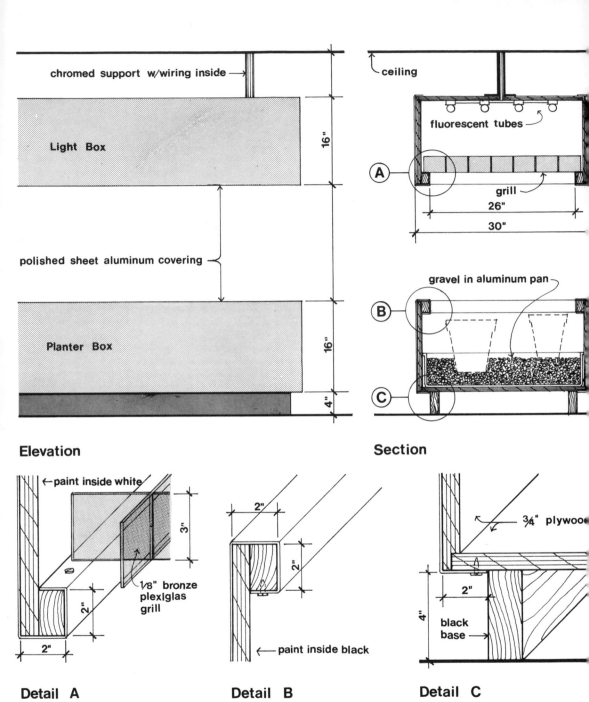

chromed support w/wiring inside →

Light Box

16"

polished sheet aluminum covering ⌐

16"

Planter Box

4"

Elevation

⌐ ceiling

fluorescent tubes ↘

Ⓐ

grill

26"

30"

gravel in aluminum pan ⌐

Ⓑ

Ⓒ

Section

←paint inside white

3"

⅛" bronze
plexiglas
grill

2"

2"

Detail A

2"

2"

← paint inside black

Detail B

¾" plywood

2"

4"

black
base →

Detail C

Planter Divider—Construction Details

Planter Divider—Perspective View

13

Five floodlights accent and help maintain these fine foliage plants in an entrance-hall corner. Ficus, philodendron and Dracaena marginata *are the plants. (Photo by General Electric Co.)*

150 to 250 watts maintain almost any foliage plant, no matter how tall. Mount lamps on a wall or ceiling, but be sure to place them 36 inches from the plant so that excessive heat will not hinder growth.

Mercury vapor lamps (see page 73) are also used for display lighting of plants. Their advantage over standard incandescent lamps is that they can be placed as far as 5 feet from the plant and still provide adequate light, because they are available in 250 watts (with special fixtures for easy home installation).

WHERE TO PUT GARDENS

Before you start indoor light gardening, decide *where* plants will be most effective in your home. Where you wish to put them will dictate what kind of setup to have. If you want a small hobby garden, fluorescent light trays, carts or built-in shelf gardens are fine. If you want decorative greenery in the living room, a large floor plant like the fiddleleaf fig (*Ficus lyrata*) is a striking accent with an incandescent floodlamp. The lamp pro-

14

Accent floodlights in handsome fixtures furnish "sunshine" for this attractive array of indoor plants. The plant on the left is schefflera; on the right is a mature specimen of Dracaena sanderiana. (*Photo courtesy Halo Lighting Co.*)

vides dramatic highlights and also furnishes growth light for the plant if it is away from windows. I feel that shelf gardens and small plants have their limitations in most interiors while display lighting with incandescent lamps and large plants is much more effective. Of course, this is a matter of personal taste.

If you want a *group of smaller display plants* rather than single plants to soften the sometimes sterile lines of a room, you can use fluorescent lamps, provided they are in attractive plant furniture. The planters probably will have to be custom designed to harmonize with room furnishings. You can design and make your own, or have them designed and made, or have someone design them and build them yourself. In any case, the planter *must* be in character with the room.

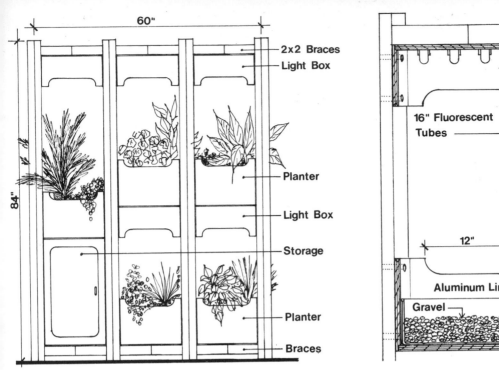

60"

2x2 Braces
Light Box

Planter

Light Box

Storage

Planter

Braces

84"

Elevation

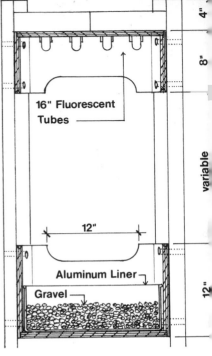

4"

8"

16" Fluorescent
Tubes

variable

12"

Aluminum Liner

Gravel

12"

Section

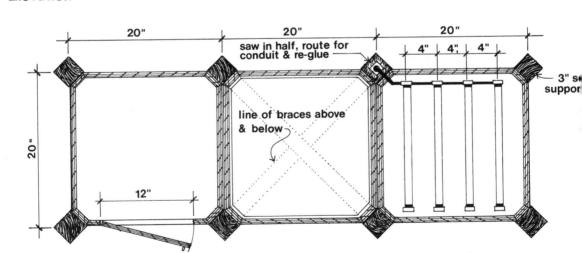

20"

20"

20"

saw in half, route for
conduit & re-glue

4" 4" 4"

3" s
suppor

line of braces above
& below

20"

12"

Storage Unit   **Planter Box**   **Light Box (underside)**

Note: boxes constructed of ¾" veneered plywood & bolted to supports

Modular Planters—Construction Details

Modular Planters—Perspective View

17

Shelf gardens can be easily constructed at home. In this bookcase arrangement two fluorescent tubes supply light for a begonia and a peperomia. (Photo by Roche)

If the garden will be in the kitchen, use two fluorescent lamps under a counter for lighting plants. These shelf gardens are ideal for small spaces, as are the better designed table units you can buy from suppliers *if they will fit* the specific space. Similarly, bathroom counter space can be used to provide greenery in otherwise useless areas.

As mentioned in the introduction, there is a difference between the kinds of plants used for shelf gardens and for accents in rooms where aesthetics are of prime importance. However, either way there is great satisfaction in growing plants under lights and knowing they will live. It is a joy to have thriving indoor plants, rather than sick ones in dim corners. Because house plants come in all sizes there are plants for almost any setup and situation.

No matter where the garden is, remember that plants will need humidity, ventilation, watering, and reasonably suitable day and night temperatures.

GETTING STARTED

Research has shown that a combination of fluorescent and incandescent light is beneficial to plant growth. Most com-

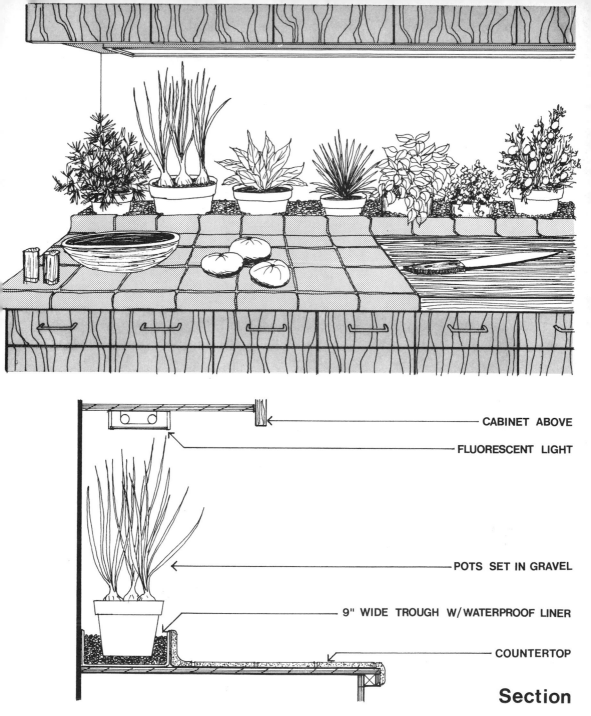

CABINET ABOVE

FLUORESCENT LIGHT

POTS SET IN GRAVEL

9" WIDE TROUGH W/WATERPROOF LINER

COUNTERTOP

Section

Countertop Plant Trough

mercial tray and cart gardens come equipped with outlets for both types of lighting and with reflector canopies. Some gardeners do not use the incandescent lamps; they rely only on fluorescents or use lamps specifically designed for plant growth, *e.g.*, Gro-Lux, Vitima, or Ultima, which manufacturers claim can be used without supplementary incandescent lighting.

If you are making your own setup, you will need reflectors to direct the light on the plants. You can buy metal reflectors, or paint the upper inside surface (where lamps are mounted) white. Fluorescent lamps come in standard lengths of 24, 48, 72, and 96 inches, in wattages ranging from 8 to 100, so plan your garden accordingly. Incandescent lamps are available in a variety of wattages, but in combination with fluorescents in shelf gardening it is best to use 15- or 20-watt lamps.

For accent and maintenance lighting of plants away from natural light sources use floodlights of 150 to 250 watts. Appropriate wall or ceiling fixtures are necessary; many are sold by suppliers. *Note:* Don't confuse accent floodlighting with combination lighting in shelf gardens. In the former, *150- to 250-watt* floods are used, in the latter, 15- or 20-watt standard bulbs.

The cost of operating fluorescent and incandescent lamps for plants varies, depending on the rate charged by the local power company. The average cost per kilowatt hour is less than 6 cents. Thus, a 100-watt setup operating for 14 hours daily (the average time period for most plants) equals 1400 watts or 1.4 kilowatts—less than 10 cents a day, which I think you'll agree is quite a bargain.

LIGHT SETUPS

Shelf Gardens
Commercial tray or cart fluorescent units are fine for beginners because they come with all the necessary hardware and lamps; just connect the unit and you are ready to grow plants

under lights. If you prefer to make your own setup to fit a specific area like a bookshelf, cupboard, or under a counter, you will need:

1. Fluorescent fixtures (fixtures that take 2 to 4 tubes are available)
2. Fluorescent lamps
3. Incandescent lamps and fixtures (optional)
4. Reflectors, metal (or white paint)
5. Lumber
6. Screws
7. Automatic timer
8. Plastic tray to protect counters

This movable fluorescent light garden is portable. Gravel-filled trays hold plants; water evaporating in the gravel helps maintain good humidity. Fixtures used include both fluorescent and supplementary incandescent light. (Photo by General Electric Co.)

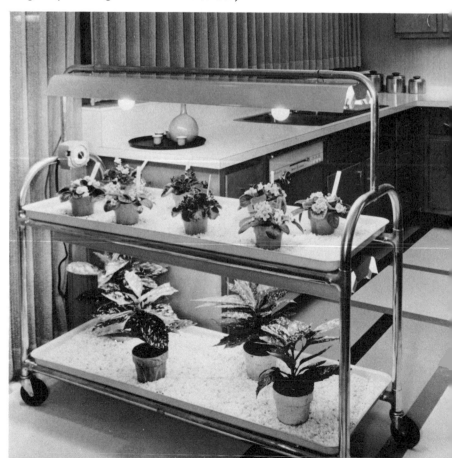

Keep plants 8 to 10 inches from light source.

In such a setup you can grow any or all the following plants:

Begonias (many kinds)
Coleus blumei (rainbow plant)
Dracaena godseffiana
Episcia dianthiflora
Gloxinias (many kinds)
Maranta leuconeura kerchoveana
Neoregelia carolinae (fire plant)
Peperomias
Philodendron soderoi
Pilea
Saintpaulia (African violets)
Syngonium podophyllum (arrowhead)

Custom Planters

A suggestion for growing large plants in living-room light gardens with fluorescent lamps is shown on pages 12 and 13. You can also use panels of fluorescents covered with grid plastic (sold at lumber yards) to diffuse the light and hide the mechanics (with these setups installation by an electrician is necessary). Plants you can grow include:

Aechmea chantini
Billbergia nutans (queen's tears)
Cissus antarctica (grape ivy)
Ferns (many kinds)
Medinilla magnifica (love plant)
Pandanus veitchii (screw pine)
Philodendron hastatum
Palms (small species)
Rechsteineria smithiantha

Display Lighting

For display and maintenance lighting with incandescent lamps of specimen or floor plants in a living room, dining room, and so forth, as shown on page 23, you will need:

1. 150- or 250-watt floodlights, incandescent or mercury vapor

2. Appropriate fixtures (bullet or canopy)
3. Ceiling track (several kinds available)
4. Timer
5. Separate circuit

In this setup you can grow large decorator plants such as:
Araucaria excelsa (Norfolk pine)
Chamaedorea erumpens (bamboo palm)
Dizygotheca elegantissima
Dracaena marginata
Dracaena massangeana (tree type)
Ficus elastica (rubber tree)
Ficus lyrata (fiddleleaf fig)
Howea forsteriana (sentry palm)
Monstera deliciosa (Swiss cheese plant)
Schefflera acontifolia (umbrella tree)

Keep plants 36 inches from light source; if you are using mercury vapor lamps, lights may be placed as much as 5 feet away from the plant.

This indoor-outdoor garden is lighted with incandescent floods; the effect is highly dramatic at night, and all plants prosper. (Photo by General Electric Co.)

2·Light, Lamps, and Plant Life

A PLANT IN A DIM CORNER may live for a few months, but it won't prosper and mature there because without sufficient light it cannot complete its life cycle. Light is necessary for photosynthesis—the production of sugar and starches from carbon dioxide and water. The duration of a plant's exposure to light (photoperiodism) determines the amount of food produced and whether a plant grows well and produces blooms.

HOW PLANTS USE LIGHT

The visible spectrum, like a rainbow, has colors ranging from red to violet. Research indicates that plants require blue, red, and far red to produce normal growth. Blue enables them to manufacture carbohydrates; the red controls assimilation and also affects the plant's response to the relative length of light and darkness; far red works in conjunction with red in several ways: it controls seed germination, stem length, and leaf size by nullifying or reversing the action of the red rays.

Plants grow best when they receive sufficient levels of blue and red light, which are in standard fluorescent lamps, and far red light, which is in incandescent bulbs. (Some studies claim that the rest of the spectrum is necessary for optimum growth, but experiments continue, and incontrovertible facts have yet to be produced.)

DURATION AND INTENSITY OF LIGHT

The dark period is a crucial time for plants, and darkness means exactly that—absolute darkness. Although we know that some plants require a short day and some a long day, and that some are flexible in their needs, or neutral, we cannot determine the exact pattern for every plant. Fortunately for indoor gardeners, most house plants—caladium, calathea, coleus, hoffmannia, hoya, ficus, dieffenbachia, to name a few—are in the neutral category and will flower and set seed without precise timing of the dark period. Commercial growers must be knowledgeable about light and bloom time for seasonal sales, but most indoor gardeners don't have to concern themselves with these technicalities.

Light intensity (measured in foot candles) is important to commercial growers because they need exact conditions for maximum production. But in the home it isn't generally necessary to bother with foot-candle units. I don't use meters to measure lamp illumination; I observe the plants. If stems are spindly and foliage lacks good color, I know the plants are not getting enough light, and if leaves show burned areas, I know the plants are getting too much light.

TIMERS

An automatic timer switch should be part of the light-garden equipment. These timers, sold under several trade names, are convenient in that you can set them for a number of specific hours and know that the lamps will turn off automatically. Normal light periods for foliage plants are 12 to 14 hours; for flowering plants use lights for 16 to 18 hours daily.

Timers are also valuable for people who are away from their indoor gardens for a few days; the daily light period can be controlled.

HOW MUCH FLUORESCENT LIGHT?

The intensity of fluorescent light given to a plant must be tempered by common sense. Following are some helpful hints for better growing: For germinating seeds and cuttings, use 10 lamp watts per square foot of growing area. For shelf-garden plants like philodendrons, African violets, and most foliage plants, use 15 watts per square foot, and for high-energy species like orchids, roses, and other flowering plants, 20 lamp watts per square foot are beneficial.

If you use incandescent light in shelf gardens to furnish the

In this handmade unit, fluorescent lamps are hidden by wooden coping. Plants are assured of good humidity because doors (right) can be opened or closed at will. (Photo courtesy Indoor Light Gardening Society of America)

This basement unit of fluorescent lamps and industrial fixtures houses dozens of thriving plants. African violets and episcias glow with color under light. (Photo by Sylvania Lighting Co.)

vital far red rays that are lacking in most conventional fluorescent lamps, try the 4:1 ratio; it has worked well for me. For example, if you have 200 watts of fluorescent light, add 50 watts of incandescent light (five 10-watt bulbs). Don't confuse these low light levels of incandescent light with accent lighting, which is different—see page 71. There were times when I increased the incandescent ratio, but this created heat that harmed the plants. The above ratios are the norm, but by no means are they set rules. Trial-and-error is part of the adventure of growing plants under lights.

If light intensity in shelf gardens proves too strong for some plants, simply move them away from the light. Set them at the end zones of the lamps, where light is less intense, or raise the adjustable reflector canopy. On the other hand, if light is not strong enough for some species, boost them closer to the light. Put the potted plant on an inverted pot, or use a lattice support.

There is no set rule for how far a plant should be from fluorescent light. As mentioned, observe your plants; they tell you when they are getting too much light (leaves are pale green) or when they are not getting enough (leaves are limp).

FLUORESCENT LAMPS

Fluorescent lamps come in a dizzying array of shapes, sizes, voltages, wattages, and temperature characteristics. Manufacturers give their lamps various trade names: Cool white, daylight, warm white, natural white, soft white, and so on. However, these names can be misleading because a natural white lamp does not duplicate the sun's light, a daylight lamp does not actually duplicate daylight, and there is no difference to the touch between a cool white and a warm white lamp.

Cool white lamps are closest in providing the kind of light— red and blue—necessary for plant growth. Daylight lamps are high in blue, but low in red, and warm white and natural white, although high in red, are deficient in blue wavelengths. Fluorescent lamps come in 20, 40, or 72 watts.

In addition to these standard fluorescent lamps, several companies have lamps designed solely for aiding plant growth: among these are Gro-Lux by Sylvania Lighting Company, Plant-Gro by Westinghouse Electric Company and Vitima by Durolite Electric Company. With these lamps, supplemental incandescent light is probably not needed because plant-growth lamps are reported to have both red and blue quotients of light.

Besides the familiar standard straight lamp, there are newer types with high output. They may be grooved (Power Groove from General Electric Company), twisted in shape (Powertwist from Durolite Electric Company); or they may show no difference in shape and be designated simply as high output (HO) or very high output (VHO).

28

Perspective View

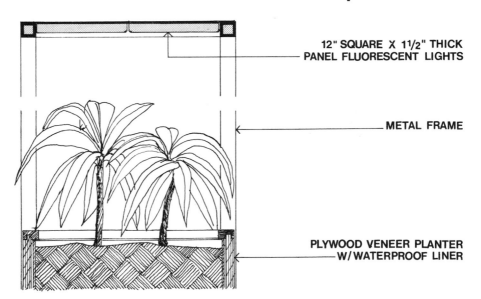

12" SQUARE X 1 1/2" THICK
PANEL FLUORESCENT LIGHTS

METAL FRAME

PLYWOOD VENEER PLANTER
W/ WATERPROOF LINER

Unit with Panel Lamps

Section

Another development in fluorescent lighting is the square panel manufactured by General Electric Company. These cool white lamps give the same light as tubular shapes but they have certain advantages: Attractive units can be created with them because the lighting mechanism is concealed, and vertical as well as horizontal lighting is possible. The panel lamp is 12 inches square and only 1½ inches thick. It fits into recessed, surface-mounted, or suspended units and comes in Panel Deluxe, Panel Deluxe Cool, and Cool White in 55 or 80 watts. The Panel Deluxe Cool type brings out vivid color hues, the closest match to natural daylight. Special ballasts are required, and installation of these lamps should be done by an electrician. Plant-to-lamp distance should be 18 to 20 inches.

The Circleline fluorescent lamps have been available for some time, but I rarely see them used. Yet they are well designed, give even illumination over a large area, and offer the only practical solution for lighting vertical setups. Somewhat like the old-fashioned fluorescent kitchen fixture, they come in 8- and 10-inch diameters. They are available in 22- or 40-watt sizes. Plant-to-lamp distance is 26 to 30 inches. Somewhat similar is the new

A portable floor cart. These commercial units come with all hardware, ready for use. This one uses only fluorescent lamps. (Photo courtesy Tube Craft Co.)

Sylvania Sun Bowl lamp with a 40-watt bulb, essentially designed for ripening fruit but also an excellent light source for dish garden arrangements.

INCANDESCENT LAMPS

Some authorities say that the major disadvantage of using incandescent lamps (reading bulbs) in plant setups is that the heat load they project can be too hot and drying for plants. This is of course unrealistic because an 8- or 15-watt lamp at a 10- or 12-inch distance does not produce enough heat to harm a plant in shelf gardens. And in accent lighting, where 150 watts are used, the lamp source is placed 30 to 36 inches from plants, so again there is no harm to plants from the heat. Incandescent lamps are more expensive to use than fluorescent lamps; 70 percent of the power that goes into an incandescent lamp is wasted. However, when used as accent lighting for plants, incandescent lamps can keep a plant in a dim spot flourishing for years, whereas otherwise it would perish. So if you have large ornamental greenery decorating your living room, incandescent flood-lighting is well worth the extra cost. With this lighting, the lamp-to-plant distance must be at least 24 to 30 inches—36 inches is an even safer distance. Mercury vapor lamps can be placed even farther away—5 to 6 feet from plants—and still furnish adequate light.

Fixtures used with incandescent lamps for accent lighting include bullet or canopy reflectors and reflector floodlights that give a directional control of light on the plant and put it on display while supplying beneficial light rays without an increase in heat. The bullet fixture is attractive and hides bare bulbs from view, and even one 150-watt lamp keeps a plant in a shaded area handsome for many months.

There is a new incandescent flood-type growing lamp now available, but so far I can find little difference between it and the ordinary incandescent flood, other than that it costs more. Manu-

Even an ordinary incandescent reading lamp will help to maintain plants in dim areas. These philodendrons are doing fine. (Photo by General Electric Co.)

facturers say these lamps have a better red-to-blue light ratio, and perhaps this is so, but I have yet to see controlled studies, although I am sure there will be more research in this area in the future.

Mercury vapor lamps embody both fluorescent lamps and incandescent elements in the same housing. There are several kinds of mercury vapor lamps; the easiest to use is a self ballasting type sold under the name Fluomeric and manufactured by the Duro-Test Corporation. No additional equipment is needed (as in fluorescent lamp installation). Mercury vapor lamps are also available under other trade names, so check with local dealers.

Use mercury vapor lamps (see page 73) as you would use incandescent floods. They diffuse light over a large area and from a considerable distance. One 150-watt flood is suitable for an area about 3 or 4 feet in diameter; mount it 5 to 6 feet from the plants.

Whichever lamps you use, remember that none are miracle workers by themselves. Plants still need water, humidity, ventilation, feeding, and pest control. Some of the lamps may be better than others for plant growth, but plants will grow and prosper under any light provided there is enough illumination and sufficient day length.

3·Growing Plants Under Fluorescent Light

HAVING PLANTS UNDER fluorescent lights is somewhat like having them in a greenhouse, but even in a protected environment plants need routine care. Plants at windows are more-or-less dormant during the gray winter months because without adequate light they manufacture little food and need less water than when they are growing in sunny summer days. But plants under lights—whether in shelf gardens or under accent lights—grow all year; photosynthesis is then the same in winter as it is in summer, so good care must be exercised. And you'll be happy to give the plants the attention they need because the reward is a beautiful garden 12 months of the year instead of merely a few months.

HUMIDITY

In recent years the need for humidity in the home—for plants, people, and even furniture—has been much publicized. House plants, like people, prefer a relative humidity of 40 to 60

33

percent. Although a few plants like a higher humidity, they too, after a time, will adapt to a lower percentage of moisture in the air. Avoid extremes; try to maintain a happy medium. Remember that the warmer and drier the air, the more humidity must be supplied to plants. At night, with cooler temperatures, don't fret if the humidity drops to 20 or 30 percent; it makes for better growth. A hygrometer, an instrument that measures the relative amount of humidity in the air, is necessary equipment for the shelf garden. It is inexpensive and available from suppliers.

In most parts of the country, humidity in summer is rarely a problem for plants, but during the winter, in cold areas where homes are artificially heated, plants are plagued by low humidity. Artificial heating dries out the air faster than we think. Because plants take up water through their roots and release it through their leaves, they give off moisture faster when the surrounding air is dry than when it is damp. When they lose water faster than they can replace it, leaves become thin and growth is spindly.

To increase the humidity in the shelf or counter garden, set the plants on a shallow tray filled with gravel that is kept moist; evaporation of the water furnishes moist air around the plants. However, this method alone will not furnish adequate humidity

In shelf units humidity is an important part of growing plants successfully. Here many plants growing together help create humidity. (Photo courtesy Westinghouse Electric Co.)

A table model fluorescent light unit is fine for a few plants. Pebbles can be put in tray to catch excess water and help create humidity. (Photo by Sylvania Electric Co.)

for most plants. Misting the foliage with tepid water is helpful in dry rooms, at least once a day in winter and much more often the rest of the year. For several years I used a 15-cent window-cleaning-fluid bottle with an attached sprayer for my indoor gardens. But today's new sprayers are better than my old-fashioned method. These hand-operated fog makers are sold under various trade names and come in 16- or 32-ounce sizes. They dispense a fine spray that covers a large area; thus, misting plants is simple. Select a good fog maker, preferably one with brass parts, so it will last a long time.

Moisture is released from leaves through transpiration, so growing many plants together helps to provide 30 to 50 percent humidity, a safe figure for most species. Enclosing a shelf garden is another method of increasing the moisture in the air, around the plants; but don't make the enclosure airtight because adequate ventilation is just as important as proper humidity. Although plastic bags can be used, a light garden draped in plastic is hardly a pleasant sight; sliding glass doors, where possible, make it attractive.

Another way to add moisture to the air is to purchase a small room humidifier. Several years ago I had a 20-inch round unit that provided a mist of cool water and a blower that circulated the mist in the growing area. This humidifier had a 1-gallon water capacity and operated for about 8 hours without refilling. The humidifier was an easy way to add moisture to the air, but since my collection of plants numbered 300, I found I didn't need it: the plants created their own humidity.

35

Don't buy vaporizers (the kind for head colds); they furnish steam rather than a cool vapor, and the steam increases the temperature, which is generally not desirable for most plants.

VENTILATION

The movement and circulation of fresh air (ventilation) is a vital part of growing plants successfully. Remember that most plants come from tropical parts of the world, where temperatures are generally 65° to 78° F. during the day and 10° less at night and where air circulation is always good. Very few plants grow in stagnant air. Good ventilation also helps prevent the development of fungus diseases, and free movement of air provides a good supply of oxygen for plant respiration.

To help the circulation of fresh air, don't crowd the plants; give each one growing space. Avoid drafts on plants; try to keep a window open near but not in the growing area. Even in winter, a window open an inch or so will help remedy a stuffy atmosphere. If all windows must be shut, a small recirculating fan operating on low speed will help provide air movement. (Try one of the new 4-inch plastic fans that operate on three speeds: low, moderate, and high.) If you are using incandescent and fluorescent lamps for plant growth, a fan set in the corner of the growing area directed at the lamps is helpful.

TEMPERATURE

Temperature and light influence the various plant-growth processes; they are the factors, along with adequate moisture, that determine whether a plant grows and blooms, remains the same, or becomes spindly. Many flowering plants set buds only when the night temperature is below 60° F. It is important that plants have a night temperature lower than during the day. Most

This unit is somewhat different from most commercial installations. The plant bin is recessed in the table and a pair of fluorescent lamps provides sufficient illumination for plants. (Photo courtesy Westinghouse Electric Co.)

species will benefit from a 10° drop; others require a drop of 15° or even 20° to really prosper. Generally my plants are grown at 62° to 76° F. by day and 60° to 65° F. at night. Some orchids and geraniums are grown cooler, about 58° F. at night. Ideally, if you grow many varieties, you should have two areas for plants: a place for warmth-loving species and a place for those plants that need coolness.

SOIL

Plants under lights deplete the natural nutrients in soil faster than plants grown at windows, because they grow faster, so start with a rich soil that contains adequate food and will sustain growth for the longest possible time.

The soil should be neither clayey (holding moisture for a long time) nor sandy (letting water go through too fast); it should be porous, with a mealy texture, like a well-done baked potato. I use 1 part garden loam to 1 part sand to 1 part leaf mold. For succulents, cacti, and a few euphorbias, I add more sand. For acid-loving plants, I add some peat moss (spongelike material

37

that absorbs and retains ten to twenty times its weight in water). Most bromeliads and orchids need osmunda fiber (chopped fern roots) or fir bark (the steamed pieces of evergreen bark); both are available at nurseries.

Commercial packaged soils have never been successful for me. You never know exactly what is in the mixture, or in what proportions the ingredients have been mixed. I buy soil by the bushel from the local greenhouse; it is the same soil growers use and contains *all* necessary ingredients.

Even though growing mediums that contain no soil, for example, Cornell University's peatlike mixtures, have some advantages (such as their light weight), they have *no* nutrients, so a careful supplemental feeding program must be followed. I have found this a tedious procedure.

POTS AND CONTAINERS

I use standard clay pots for growing plants under lights; they come in many sizes, are inexpensive, and I know from experience how long it takes the moisture to be absorbed through the clay walls. Plastic pots, which retain moisture longer, are lightweight, do not encourage the formation of algae, and if dropped rarely break. And, too, it is not necessary to water plants in plastic pots as often as when they are in standard clay containers.

POTTING

Potting is the first planting of a seedling or a cutting in a container; repotting is the transfer of a plant from one pot to a larger one. Select containers neither too large nor too small in relation to the size of the plant (always start very small for cuttings and go no more than 2 inches larger for repotting).

To pot or repot a plant, start with a clean container; if it is a

One floodlight illuminates this lovely built-in custom floor unit. Gravel is used as a base and also to help provide some humidity as excess water evaporates from the stones. (Photo courtesy General Electric Co.)

new clay pot, soak it overnight or the pot will draw moisture from the soil of the new planting. Put one or two broken pieces of clay pot over the drainage hole. Pour in a few porous stones like perlite and a few granules of charcoal to keep the soil sweet. Add a mound of fresh soil, about 2 inches. Place the plant in the center of the container, and fill in and around it with fresh soil. Strike the base of the pot on the table a few times to settle the soil and to eliminate air gaps. When repotting, tamp down soil around the edge of the pot with a flat stick or pencil so that new soil surrounds the root ball and gets beneath it. Remember to leave an inch of space at the top between the pot rim and the soil to receive water. Drench newly potted plants, and let them dry out for a few days in a shaded place. Then place them under lights and start regular waterings.

I am often asked when to repot plants; there is no definite answer. Repotting depends on the type of container used, how much water and light you give, the soil, and how much feeding the plants are given. Repot less frequently than you think necessary—the best indicator is when roots come out of the bottom of the container.

WATER

Plants under lights dry out faster than plants at windows. Quite possibly you'll have to water every other day in autumn and winter and daily in spring and summer, but this depends on the kind of plant. Some species like to be thoroughly dry between waterings, others want to be just evenly moist, and a few like to be wet at all times. But whatever the situation, when you water, do it thoroughly. Allow excess water to pour through the drainage hole so that the complete root system gets moisture. If the top of the soil stays wet and the lower part remains dry, the soil generally turns sour and growth is retarded or stops completely.

Once a month, if possible, soak plants in a pail of water at the sink or stand them in a bathtub. Set the pots in water to the rim for about an hour or longer so that accumulated acids and salts from fertilizers that can harm plants are dissolved.

FEEDING

I have successfully grown many window plants without too much supplemental feeding. However, plants under lights usually need additional feeding on a regular schedule. Nutrients are depleted quickly, and plants simply will not grow without having these nutrients replenished. In summer, generally feed plants every other watering, and the rest of the year feed them about every third watering. Do follow instructions on package or bottle.

Commercial fertilizers (foods) contain nitrogen, phosphorous, and potash; the ratio of elements is marked on the bottle or package in this order. Select a fertilizer carefully; don't buy just anything. Foliage plants do best with a high nitrogen solution. I use 20–10–10 for them. Flowering plants do better with 10–10–5; too much nitrogen can impede or stop bud formation.

New plants and ailing plants don't need feeding. New ones in fresh soil have enough nutrients for 2 months or more; ailing plants are not capable of absorbing nutrients. After plants bloom, allow them to rest a few weeks with only an occasional watering. Start feeding again in about 6 weeks. A safe rule to follow is to fertilize plants when they show new growth (usually in spring).

40

4·Plants for Shelf Gardening

FOR SUCCESSFUL GROWING, start with plants that need low-light intensity. Foliage plants like philodendrons, scheffleras, and dieffenbachias are handsome ornamentals and thrive under lights with little care. Begonias and gesneriads, including the popular African violets, are well-known "light" plants that are the back-bone of a good collection because they offer limitless color all year. Miniature succulents and cacti are other good possibilities; I have several dish gardens of them, far superior to the cacti grown in the garden room. Most miniature and dwarf geraniums, too, can be grown under lights provided they are in coolness, and although several orchids and bromeliads will not respond under artificial light, there are many that do.

For me it has been easier to have two medium-sized light gardens than one large one. I group foliage plants, gesneriads, and some begonias in one tray; geraniums, orchids, and bromeliads are in the other growing area. If you are limited to one garden, put the plants that need strong light (geraniums, etc.) in the center where the light is brightest and the other plants at the ends of the lamps where light is less intense.

In many of my growing arrangements, I keep night temperatures between 52° and 60° F. Of course, like all gardeners, I can't restrict myself to a certain number of plants. I am forever adding charming ferns, too-tall banana plants, and even carnivorous species, first trying them in one place in the garden and then

41

moving them about until I find a place where they respond. Plants themselves will give you the clues: fresh growth, new buds. Experimenting is fun, but once a plant starts to respond in one location, leave it there.

Rosette-type plants grow better under lights than, say, trailers and hanging species. It is difficult to train trailing plants in shelf units, and although it is often suggested that you let them climb the posts or bracing, it has never worked well for me because they eventually become tangled in the bracework and rarely look attractive. However, they can certainly be grown in light gardens until they become too large, and then moved to pedestals for room decoration. Large podocarpus, dieffenbachias, or other tall vertical plants are better grown as accent plants (see Chapter 5). Seedlings and cuttings do better under lamps than they do in natural light.

When placing plants under lights, keep in mind that the plants at each end of the lamps grow more slowly than those in the center. Never replace all the lamps at one time. Put in one, wait a day, then put in another to avoid shocking plants with an abundance of new light.

Start plants rather far away, 10 to 12 inches, and gradually raise them, or lower the lamps after a few weeks; experiment and observe. If the leaves are light green or yellow-green, the plant is getting too much light; raise the lamps. If growth is spindly and stems are elongated, lower the lamps. Decreasing the distance from plant to lamp gives twice as much light, in the case of incandescents, as in that of fluorescents.

With gardening under lights, all cultural factors—humidity, temperature, moisture, and ventilation—must be considered. Each aspect of growing is dependent on the others. When you arrive at the right set of conditions, in other words, when the growing elements are balanced, flourishing plants are your reward.

GARDEN SETUPS

As mentioned before, the fluorescent light garden may be either a commercial unit or a handcrafted setup. What you choose depends on the place where the garden is to be and just how much gardening you want to do. In addition to the commercial units, we offer drawings of some unique ways to have plants under lights in your home: a freestanding metal unit, a wall niche arrangement, and an attractive bookcase setup. In all these gardens, use small or medium (12- to 30-inch) plants. Larger plants (specimen plants) for accent lighting are discussed in Chapter 5.

PLANTS FOR SHELF GARDENS

Begonias

This is a versatile plant family for indoor growing. Most begonias like rex and the hirsute (hairy-leaved) types can be grown under a two-lamp setup. Others, like angel wings, semperflorens (wax begonias), and rhizomatous begonias, need more light, so a four-lamp arrangement is best if you want abundant flowers. The rhizomatous and hirsute species bear tall spikes of spring and summer bloom; the semperflorens produce almost year-round color under lights. For foliage it is difficult to find more attractive plants than rex begonias, with their leaves that appear like tapestry; under artificial light, they glow. If space is limited, try miniatures; they are truly charming.

When grown at windows, many begonias have a dormant period, but under lights most grow all year. However, as with all plants, a slight rest of 3 to 4 weeks, immediately after flowering, with less water than usually given, is prudent culture. Cooler nights and less light are also recommended after plants have finished bloom.

Place rex, rhizomatous, and hairy-leaved begonias 12 to 14

Perspective View

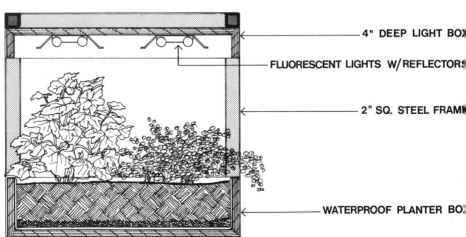

4" DEEP LIGHT BOX

FLUORESCENT LIGHTS W/REFLECTORS

2" SQ. STEEL FRAME

WATERPROOF PLANTER BOX

Freestanding Metal Unit

Section

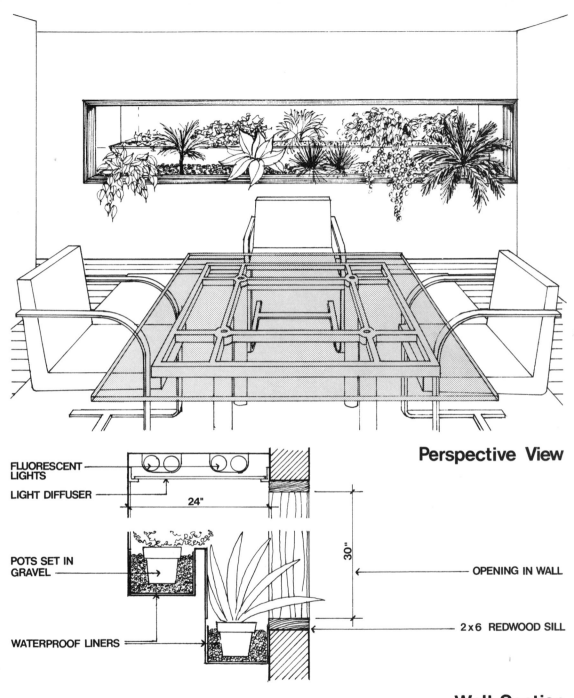

Perspective View

FLUORESCENT LIGHTS

LIGHT DIFFUSER

24"

POTS SET IN GRAVEL

30"

OPENING IN WALL

WATERPROOF LINERS

2 x 6 REDWOOD SILL

Wall Niche Planter

Wall Section

45

Perspective Vie

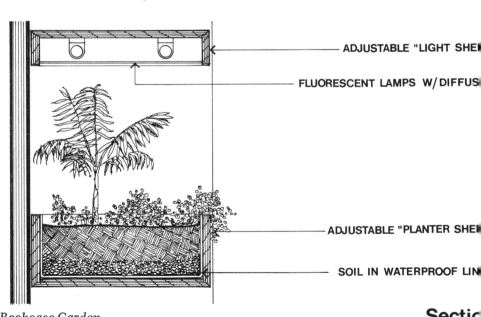

ADJUSTABLE "LIGHT SHE**

FLUORESCENT LAMPS W/DIFFUS**

ADJUSTABLE "PLANTER SHE**

SOIL IN WATERPROOF LIN**

Bookcase Garden

Sectio

46

inches from the lamps, with 10 to 12 hours of light, because too much illumination bleaches the leaves. Angel wings and semperflorens need high light intensity of 14 to 16 hours daily to be at their best. Place them about 8 to 12 inches from the lamps.

Rex. To 18 inches tall. The colored foliage of rex begonias makes them preferred plants, and even though they may be temperamental at windows, they grow easily under lights. Use small containers of rich soil that drains readily. Do not keep the plants overly moist; allow them to dry out between waterings. Keep humidity at a moderate level, 30 to 50 percent, and mist the area around the pots, but don't let excess moisture accumulate on the leaves. Average home temperatures suit rex begonias: 70° to 74° F. by day and about 64° F. at night. Don't feed them too much; once every third watering has produced lush growth for my plants.

> 'Black Diamond'. Dark maroon, center zone burnished silver.
> 'Cardoza Gardens'. Purple, silver, and green foliage; brilliant.
> 'Fiesta'. Round leaves splashed with silver and pink.
> 'Glory of St. Albans'. Metallic rose-purple leaves.
> 'Helen Teupel'. Silver and maroon foliage.
> 'Merry Christmas'. Striped with color, mostly red.
> 'Peace'. Metallic red and silver foliage.
> 'Thrush'. Crimson-red leaves dotted silver.
> 'Winter Queen'. Spiral-form leaf, silver, purple, and pink.

Hirsute. To 24 inches tall. These fine plants grow well with less humidity and slightly less moisture than the rex varieties. They also tolerate coolness better than most begonias because the hairy coats on their leaves keep them warm. Use a somewhat rich soil, but don't repot them too often; once every third year is best. In a few years the plants grow into lovely specimens, at which point I take them from the light garden and use them as coffee-table or entry-hall decoration. Will need moderate light in the indoor garden.

> 'Alleryi'. Frosted green leaves accented with purple; pale-pink
>   flowers.
> 'Alto Scharff'. Fuzzy green leaves; pink blooms edged with red.

47

B. *incana* (*peltata*). Fleshy green leaves; white blooms. Unique.

B. *luxurians*. Gray-green palmlike leaves.

B. *metallica*. Silver, dark green and purple hairy leaves; pink blooms.

B. *scharffii* (*haageana*). Large olive-green foliage; pink-and-white flowers.

B. *venosa*. Green cupped leaves.

'Viaude'. Cupped olive-green leaves; bearded white flowers.

'Zuensis'. Reddish-green leaves; hairy pink blooms.

Angel wing. To 30 inches tall. Perhaps the most showy in the group, angel wings are always lovely, but under lights they grow and grow and become so tall so quickly that they can be a problem. A large angel wing is a good accent plant. Give them intense light and an evenly moist soil. They will grow lavishly with average home temperatures and humidity, about 30 percent. Feed only moderately.

'Alzasco'. Dark-green leaves spotted with silver; red flowers.

'Argentea Guttata'. Creamy flowers tinged white.

B. *coccinea*. Bright-green shiny leaves; red or pink varieties.

'Di-Erna'. Blooms freely with coral blooms.

'Grey Feather'. Slim, dark green almost gray leaves; white flowers.

'Pink Spot Lucerne'. Green and pink foliage; red flowers.

'Sylvan Grandeur'. Multicolored leaves; pink blooms.

Semperflorens. To 16 inches tall. The improvement in wax begonias is amazing. Once they were only for outdoor garden beds; now, with the new improved hybrids of double flowers, they are worth space in the light garden. They grow, bloom, rest a bit, and then repeat the cycle. After they flower, it's a good idea to cut them back somewhat so they stay bushy and bloom abundantly. Don't overwater; keep them just barely moist all year. Will take considerable light. Place 2 to 4 inches from lamps.

'Ballet'. Double white blossoms, with striking bronze leaves.

'Cinderella'. Crested pink blooms tipped with red.

'Dainty Maid'. Cupped green leaves; white blooms.

'Firefly'. Crested fiery-red flowers.

'Lucy Locket'. Double pink flowers.

'Winkie'. Dark-green foliage; rose flowers.

48

Robust African violets thrive in this fluorescent light garden; heat and humidity are closely regulated; white reflectors throw light evenly on plants; note thermometer hanging from top shelf. (Photo by Matthew Barr)

Tuberous. Many growers suggest the lovely tuberous varieties for fluorescent gardens, but I tried them several times and found that their need for a combination of high humidity and cool nights makes them difficult indoor plants. By all means start them in the light garden, 4 to 6 inches from tubes, but once they are growing transfer them to outdoor pots for maximum bloom.

    'Black Knight'. Deep crimson flowers.
    'Flambeau'. Double orange-scarlet blooms.

49

'Mandarin'. Double salmon-orange flowers.
'Copper Gold'. Multiflora type; double gold.
'Helen Harms'. Multiflora type; double yellow.
'Sweet Home'. Multiflora type, double red.
'Tasso'. Multiflora type; semidouble pink.

Miniature. To 12 inches tall. I sometimes believe these plants were made especially for growing under lights. They give an enormous reward for very little effort, and they are always colorful and generous with flowers. At the start it takes them a few months to adjust to artificial light, but once growing they need little care. Keep the plants about 14 to 16 inches from the lamps; provide an evenly moist soil and 30 to 50 percent humidity. I grow my miniatures with 16 hours of light.

> *B. ardicaulis.* Tiny green leaves; white blooms.
> *B. boweri.* Immensely popular. Green leaves stitched wtih black at edges. Several good varieties.
> 'Chantilly Lace'. Cupped leaves, eyelash hairs at edges; pink blooms.
> 'Lulandi'. Bright-green foliage; large pink flowers.
> 'Orange Dainty'. A real gem; dark-green leaves and orange blooms.
> 'Red Berry'. Fine rex with wine-red foliage.
> 'Red Wing'. Another good rex; wine-red leaves, silver edges.
> 'Rosa Kugel'. A wax begonia with small green leaves.
> 'Virbob'. Multicolored leaves; pink flowers.

Rhizomatous. To 30 inches tall. A group of fascinating diverse begonias, some small, others medium-sized, and still others large. Leaves may be round or star-shaped, with plain or fancy patterns. Leaf texture may be satiny, smooth, or nubby, and the foliage may be frilled or stained with brocaded colors. The rhizomes skim the surface of the soil; they should not be buried when you pot the plants. The rhizomes also act as water storehouses if you forget to water the plants. Use shallow pots; rhizomes don't have extensive root systems, and unused soil can create sour conditions. Let plants dry out thoroughly between waterings. Some varieties will take a short rest in winter, but others grow all year. Feed moderately. Provide average humidity and moderate to intense light.

50

'Beatrice Haddrell'. Star-shaped dark-green, almost black, foliage;
   pink blooms.
'Bunchi'. Light- or dark-green leaves; shell-pink blooms.
'Crestabruchi'. Unique, with heavily ruffled twisted-edged leaves.
   Pink flowers.
B. *decora.* Brownish-green leaves etched with chartreuse veins;
   white flowers.
'Erythrophylla'. Also known as 'Feasti'. Round leaves, green on
   top, red underneath; pink flowers.
B. *hemsleyana.* Green leaves that grow in an umbrella pattern;
   lovely pink blooms.
'Maphil'. Also sold as 'Cleopatra'; gold, chocolate-brown, and
   chartreuse leaves; tiny pink flowers.
'Ricinifolia'. Leaves like those of the castor-bean plant.
B. *strigilosa.* Chocolate-brown spotted green leaves on long graceful stems. Blush-white flowers.
B. *vellosoana.* Iridescent leaves, chartreuse veined, glow in
   fluorescent light.

Cacti and Succulents

Cacti and succulents have never been the favorites in my
plant room; there they showed little growth and scanty flowering.
However, under lights they have taken on new interest for me.
Many of them bloom and growth is accelerated, and so they join
the ranks of exciting indoor plants. Some of these plants are from
the desert, where there are long periods of extreme heat and
drought. They have evolved to the stage where they have small
leaves and coverings of fleshy stems, spines, or scales to lessen
moisture evaporation. All cacti are succulents, but not all succulents are cacti. Rebutia, Echinocereus, Mammillaria, and
Opuntia are examples of desert cacti that need a soil mix of equal
parts sand and garden loam. Average daytime home temperatures (65° to 80° F.) suit most cacti and succulents. In winter
most need a rest, so water them only about once a week; also give
them lower night temperatures (say, 10° lower) and short light
duration, not more than 8 hours.

Jungle species like Epiphyllum and Schlumbergera are best
grown in equal parts of rich soil and shredded osmunda kept
evenly moist. In winter, give them coolness, about 60° F., and less

water; limit light duration to about 9 hours if you want them to set buds. Any interruption of the important night period—even lamplight from across the street—will retard or completely hinder flowering.

Cacti and succulents don't grow rapidly, so feed them moderately, about once a month. Grow the desert species 2 to 4 inches from the lamps, giving them light 14 to 16 hours daily (except in winter when 8 to 10 hours daily is sufficient); grow the jungle types (epiphytes) 6 to 12 inches from lamps with light for 12 to 14 hours daily.

Cacti

Astrophytum myriostigma. Dark-green-dotted white; yellow flowers.

Echinocereus. Ribbed globe with white to purple flowers.

Echinopsis calochlora. Yellow-brown cactus wtih white blooms.

E. eyriesii. Small white flowers; brown spines.

Lobivia aurea. Dark-green globular plant with yellowish-brown spines.

L. backebergii. Pale-green globe; brown spines; red blooms.

L. cylindrica. Small deep-green plant; white and brown needles.

L. larabei. Cluster plant. Red flowers.

L. rossii. Globular; red flowers.

Mammillaria baumii. Elongated glossy green globe with white spines.

M. elongata. Light-green cylinders with yellow spines; white flowers.

M. multiceps. Dark-green globe; salmon flowers.

Notocactus apricus. Dark-green globe; bristly spines and yellow blooms.

N. concinnus. Glossy green and depressed globe; red and yellow blooms.

N. mammulosus. Shiny green with yellow blooms.

N. ottonis. Glossy green globe; yellow blooms.

N. scopa. Silvery green cylindrical plant with yellow flowers.

Succulents

Adromischus maculatus. Rosette with gray-green flat leaves.

Aloe variegata. Triangular blue-green leaves marked with white.

Crassula deceptrix. Clustered and stubby thick silver-gray leaves with brown dots.

C. falcata. Wide, flat, and curved gray-green leaves.

C. schmidtii. Small gray-green needlelike leaves; red flowers.
C. teres. Closely pressed green leaves with white margin.
C. triebneri. Pointed green leaves marked with darker green.
Delosperma echinatum. Small green leaves; yellow flowers.
Echeveria crenulata. 'Rosen Grandis'. Rich green, waxy leaves
    tipped red.
Euphorbia obesa. Small gray-green globes.
Kleinia articulata. Waxy green stems with bluish leaves; white
    flowers.
Sedum morganianum. Good for hanging basket. Silvery green
    foliage; red flowers.

Bromeliads

These plants are almost indestructible. They will grow for months without light, but it is only when they have sufficient light that the true brilliance of their foliage can be appreciated. There are epiphytic and terrestrial bromeliads; both succeed in a mixture of equal parts shredded osmunda and soil. Keep center of plants filled with water, with the potting mix just barely moist. The beauty of bromeliads lies in their bright, spectacularly colored bracts that are vibrant for 6 months: cerise, violet, chartreuse, scarlet, and green-black. Flowers are small and hidden within the bracts.

Feed the plants only moderately because even under lights they object to too much fertilizer. You can throw away your insecticides too because the leaves are just too tough for insects.

Most bromeliads are tubular in growth or shaped with leaves in a rosette; the majority are too large for the average light garden, but there are some medium-sized species that you might want to try. Give bromeliads intense light (use four fluorescents) and keep them about 4 to 6 inches from the lamps.

Aechmea. To 30 inches tall. Mostly vase-shaped plants with brilliantly colored leaves—variegated, deep red, some appearing lacquered. Many bear red or blue berries that last for several months. Most species bloom in spring or summer, a few in winter.

    A. calyculata. To 20 inches. Crowns of vivid yellow flowers in
        April.

53

A. *fasciata*. A 24- to 30-inch favorite. Tufted blue and pink flower
heads in spring.

A. *racinae*. To 14 inches. Red, black, and yellow flowers at
Christmas.

Billbergia. To 30 inches tall. Mostly tubular plants with gray-
green, silver-green, or striped leaves. Bizarre flowers in bright
colors, but blooms last only a few days.

B. *amoena*. To 16 inches. Shiny green leaves; rose bracts in
spring or summer.

B. *nutans*. To 30 inches. An old favorite, blooming at Christmas
with chartreuse, pink, and cerise flowers.

B. *pyramidalis concolor*. To 30 inches. Golden-green leaves;
orange-pink flower crowns in summer.

Neoregelia. To 30 inches round. At bloom time plants have brilliant red centers that glow with color for many months. They
take a great deal of space, but they are appealing house plants.

N. *carolinae*. Dark green and copper leaves; winter-blooming.

N. *spectabilis*. The painted fingernail plant. Tips of pale-green
leaves turn brilliant red at bloom time in summer.

Tillandsia. To 20 inches tall. Carefree plants with palmlike
foliage or tufted growth. Most of the smaller species mentioned
here must be grown on slabs of osmunda. More curiosities than
decorative house plants.

T. *cyanea*. For pot culture. Dark-green palm leaves and purple
flowers in fall that look like butterflies.

T. *ionanthe*. To 3 inches. A tufted beauty, with red and violet
blooms in summer.

T. *juncea*. To 12 inches. Yellow and red flowers in summer.

Vriesia. To 30 inches tall. Feathery plumes of vibrant color that
last for several months make these desirable plants. Leaves are
pale green or dark green marked and banded in brown.

V. *malzinei*. To 12 inches. Green leaves; spatula-shaped orange
flower crowns.

V. *splendens*. The flaming sword plant. To 20 inches. Green
foliage with brown stripes; orange "swords" on erect stems.

54

Ferns

Ferns offer a dazzling array of foliage accent. Some have wild, bold fronds, others, with their lacy fronds, are fragile in appearance. In their natural outdoor habitat ferns grow in shady, moist, and cool locations.

The selection of ferns is bewildering; one mail-order house lists more than forty different kinds. The Boston fern is perhaps the most popular, but ferns like rabbit's-foot and bird's-nest are just as appealing.

Give ferns a very porous soil of equal parts loam, leaf mold, and sand, and keep them moist but never soggy. I don't feed ferns because fertilizer can burn leaf tips, and plants grow better without additional feeding.

Ferns should rest in winter, so decrease moisture and light; keep the soil barely moist. Plants prefer to be grown in small pots and disturbed as little as possible. If you can, put the pots on pebbles in trays to provide adequate moisture—50 percent humidity is ideal. Use large ferns for accent plants, but for the shelf garden stick to small plants. Plants need a two-lamp setup; place them 6 to 8 inches from light.

> *Adiantum cuneatum.* Old favorite. Dark-green fronds; many varieties, including *A. cuneatum excelsum*, 'Goldelse', 'Matador'. All are good and are tolerant of adverse conditions.
>
> *A. hispidulum.* Dwarf maidenhair fern; charming.
>
> *A. tenurum wrightii.* Typical maidenhair; one of the best.
>
> *Asplenium nidus.* The bird's-nest fern. Evergreen fronds. Outstanding.
>
> *A. viviparum.* Very lacy fronds; produces plantlets on leaves.
>
> *Blechnum brasiliense.* Coarse fronds; low-growing. Different.
>
> *Davallia fejeenisis.* The rabbit's-foot fern. Fine feathery foliage and hairy creeping rootstalks. A curiosity.
>
> *Nephrolepis exaltata.* The sword fern. Long pendant fronds; easy to grow. Robust.
>
> *N. exaltata* 'Fluffy Ruffles'. Heavily ruffled one; choice.
>
> *N. e.* 'Verona'. Lacy in appearance; compact growth.
>
> *Phyllitis scolopendrium.* Wide, pale-green fronds.
>
> *Platycerium bifurcatum.* The staghorn fern. Drooping fronds. Grow on rafts of osmunda.

55

P. pumila. Upright fronds in fan shape; grow on rafts of osmunda.

Polypodium polycarpon. The strap-leaf fern. Best grown on slab
of osmunda.

Polystichum (*Aspidium tsus-simense*). An ideal dwarf fern.

P. setosum. Stiff, glossy green fronds; compact growth.

Pteris ensiformis 'Victoriae'. Many forms; this one silver and
green.

Selaginella kraussiana. Bright green mossy plant.

Woodwardia orientalis. The chain fern. Excellent for basket
growing.

Geraniums

Geraniums can be grown with orchids and bromeliads in a
four- or six-lamp arrangement with supplemental incandescent
light. They can be grown with less light than this, but then they
won't produce their handsome flowers. Most geraniums thrive at
average home temperature by day (70° to 76° F.), but at night
they do need coolness, say 55° to 60° F.

Give plants a porous soil that drains readily and is somewhat
acid (pH 6.5); water them only when the soil feels dry to the
touch. Provide 40 to 60 percent humidity and apply fertilizer
about every other watering. Watch the leaves to determine if
they are not getting enough light. Spindly stems, weak growth,
and leaves that are not fully extended and seem crumpled are
signs of not enough illumination.

As stated, geraniums need intense light, so use four to six
lamps and place plants close to the lamps, about 2 to 4 inches,
for 14 to 18 hours daily. The following are some miniature
species:

'Aldebaran'. Small dark green leaves marked with black-green;
pink flowers.

'Allair'. Intense green foliage; pink blooms.

'Bumble Bee'. Dark-green leaves; red flowers.

'Capella'. Forest-green foliage; pink blooms.

'Epsilon'. Green foliage; pink flowers.

'Fairy Princess'. Dark leaves; creamy pink blooms.

'Fleurette'. Startling dark-green leaves; salmon flowers.

'Imp'. Dark foliage; salmon-pink flowers.

'Lilliput Lemon'. Lemon-scented waxy leaves.
'Moonbeam'. Dark foliage; orange blooms.
'North Star'. White with pink veins. Good accent plant.
'Polaris'. Dark-green foliage; pink-edged white flowers.
'Salmon Comet'. Black-green leaves; salmon blooms.
'Sparkle'. Dark foliage; red flowers.
'Tangerine'. Free-blooming salmon.
'Tweedledee'. Scalloped leaves; salmon blooms.

Gesneriads

These popular plants are superlative performers in the light garden. Of course, African violets are well known, but others like Aeschynanthus, Columnea, Kohleria, Hypocyrta, Episcia, Rechsteineria, Smithiantha, and Streptocarpus are certainly rewarding plants too. For colorful flowers, gesneriads take the spotlight indoors. Some orchids and geraniums may be reluctant to bloom, but gesneriads bloom their heads off!

Generally these are day-neutral plants that don't need a precise number of hours of light and dark to prosper. Their night-temperature requirements are not exacting: 60° to 65° F. will suit most varieties. Give gesneriads a porous, well-drained soil and feed them every other watering. Provide good ventilation for them because they don't like a stuffy atmosphere. Humidity of 40 to 50 percent will make your plants flourish.

Most of the gesneriads—Episcia, African violets—need medium light. Columnea, Kohleria, and Aeschynanthus do better with somewhat more illumination. Light from 14 to 16 hours makes my gesneriads thrive, and they are placed 4 to 8 inches from the lamps. I use a four-lamp setup.

Achimenes

'Blue Star'. Pale to dark-blue flowers with white eyes.
'Charm'. Floriferous; coral-pink blooms.
'Dazzler'. Small ovate leaves; large red flowers.
'Leonora'. Dark-green foliage; violet-purple blooms.
'Violetta'. Dark-green leaves; almost purple flowers.

Aeschynanthus

Aeschynanthus lobbianus. Shiny dark-green leaves; scarlet blooms.

A. pulcher. Green leaves; scarlet flowers.

A. speciosus. The lipstick vine. Shiny green leaves; orange flowers.

Columnea

Columnea arguta. Trailing vine with pointed leaves; red flowers.

'Canary'. Cornell hybrid; upright growth, yellow blooms.

'Cornellian'. Floriferous; orange flowers.

C. hirta. Three-inch orange blooms; vining growth.

C. microphylla. Long trailing stems with button leaves; burnt-red flowers.

C. 'Stavanger'. European hybrid; bright-red blooms.

Episcia

Episcia acajou. Silver foliage; red flowers.

E. cupreata. Hairy copper leaves; red blooms. Many forms.

E. lilacina. Bronze leaves; blue flowers.

'Yellow Topaz'. Green foliage; yellow flowers.

Kohleria

Kohleria allenii. Hairy leaves; red and yellow flowers.

K. amabilis. Velvety green leaves; pink flowers with purple dots.

K. bogotensis. Speckled leaves; red and yellow blooms.

K. eriantha. Bright red tubular flowers.

K. hirsuta. Hairy foliage; red blooms with pale throat.

Rechsteineria

Rechsteineria cardinalis. Small, green, velvety leaves; scarlet tubular flowers.

R. leucotricha. Large leaves covered with silver hairs; coral blooms.

R. macropoda. Bright-green leaves; small red flowers.

Sinningia

'Buell's Blue Slipper'. Velvety foliage; blue flowers.

'Defiance'. Large leaves; dark crimson flowers with waxy edges.

'Emperor Frederick'. Upright; dark ruby-red blooms bordered with white.

'Emperor William'. Large leaves; violet-blue flowers, white border.

'Pink Slipper'. Light-green leaves; rosy pink flowers with dark centers.

'Switzerland'. Soft leaves; scarlet flowers, edged white.

Smithiantha

Smithiantha cinnabarina. Nodding scarlet-red flowers.

'Golden King'. Golden-yellow flowers.

S. multiflora. Soft hairy plant; white blooms.

'Orange King'. Orange-red flowers.

'Rose Queen'. Rose-pink flowers.

S. zebrina. Leaves covered with silky hairs; red flowers.

Streptocarpus

Streptocarpus rexii. Pale-blue flowers; many forms with pink, blue, white, or purple blooms.

S. saxorum. Dark-green leaves; white and lavender flowers.

Marantas and Calatheas

Like most of our familiar house plants, the marantas are decorative plants native to the tropics. Although the family is not large (only about 200 species), it is confusing. The group also includes calatheas and ctenanthes. No matter how they are listed in catalogs (and listings will vary) these are superlative foliage plants under lights. The leaves have a crinkly texture and are beautifully marked in olive green or brown with undersides of magenta purple.

Keep the soil a bit on the wet side during the summer and evenly moist the rest of the year. The plants are at home in warmth—never less than 58° F. at night—and require 30 to 50 percent humidity. Give them a porous soil of 2 parts peat moss, 1 part sand, and 1 part loam. A few species have a dormant period and then require a soil that is barely wet.

You may have to search for a few of the species described here. Only popular ones are being offered by nurseries, but I'm sure we will see more of them in the near future. Most are small, low-growing plants, ideal for a two-lamp shelf garden; give them

59

14 to 16 hours of light, 4 to 6 inches from lamps.

Calathea argyraea. Silver-gray and green.

C. concinna. Dark-green leaves with feather design.

C. insignis. Light green with olive-green markings.

C. lietzei. Light-green feather design, purple underneath.

C. makoyana. Olive-green, pink, silver, and green foliage. Outstanding.

C. ornata 'Roseolineata'. Pink and white stripes. Striking.

C. ornata v. sanderiana. Dark, waxy foliage heavily marked with shades of green.

C. veitchiana. Iridescent leaves.

C. zebrina. Dark, velvety purple leaves with chartreuse markings.

Ctenanthe 'Burle Marx'. Gray-green and dark-green leaves.

Ctenanthe oppenheimiana. Silver and green leaves.

Maranta bicolor. Dark-green, grayish, and green leaves.

M. erytheneura. Bright-red veins on pearl-gray background.

M. leuconeura massangeana. Pearl-gray and green foliage.

Miniature Orchids

On a winter morning it is hard to beat miniature orchids at a window. They are cheerful and colorful; and even though they are not as easily grown as their larger relatives, they do indeed bloom indoors. Miniature orchids take more time to adjust to new conditions than do most plants: 3 to 5 months (depending upon the species) to regain vigor and to show new growth. Once established they come on strong.

For most of these plants you will need 2- or 3-inch pots; slotted clay pots are best. For some orchids you will have to buy rafts (solidified pieces of osmunda or tree fern). Larger orchids require a definite rest sometime during their growing cycle, but miniatures need moisture all year. There are a few exceptions and these are noted in descriptions. With rafts you must devise some method of catching dripping water; use pans or clay saucers set on cork mats to protect furniture. Don't set potted orchids on a solid surface; they need bottom ventilation. Place redwood strips 1 inch apart on clay saucers or use pans containing gravel, with wood strips over the pans and put plants on the strips. In either case, protect furniture tops with cork mats under trays or saucers.

60

Use a four-lamp setup; place plant 4 to 6 inches from lamps.

Angraecum compactum. Dark green straplike foliage; large white flowers 3 inches across.

Ascocentrum ampullaceum. Dark-green leaves; erect spikes of cerise flowers.

A. miniatum. Straplike dark-green foliage; spikes of orange blooms.

Campenemia uliginosa. Solitary cactuslike fleshy leaves; small white scented flowers.

Cattleya walkeriana. Leathery green leaves; 3-inch rose-colored flowers.

Epidendrum lindleyanum. Leafy stems; lavender flowers in autumn.

E. polybulbon. Leaves on a creeping rhizome; brownish-yellow flowers with white heart-shaped lip.

E. porpax. Tiny, oval green leaves; brownish-purple flowers of waxy texture.

Kerfersteinia gramineus. One-inch yellowish-green flowers with brownish-red spots.

Leptotes bicolor. Succulent foliage; large white-stained, deep violet flowers.

Masdevalia schroederiana. Dark-green foliage; helmet-shaped deep red flowers with spurs.

M. simula. Grassy foliage; diminutive greenish-yellow flowers dotted brilliant red.

Ornithocephalus bicornis. Leathery leaves in rosette growth; bell-shaped greenish-white blooms. Best grown on raft.

Orthochilus fuscus. Leathery pendant leaves; small bearded yellow and red blooms. Best grown on raft.

Pholidota articulata. Cascading flower spike with ½-inch yellow-white flowers.

P. chinensis. Creamy white flowers evenly spaced on a pendant stem. Best grown on raft.

Platyclinis cornuta. Solitary leaves; white flowers on a short scape. Best grown on raft.

P. filiforme (Dendrochilum filiforme). Grassy foliage; tiny yellow flowers.

Pleuorothallis aribuloides. Spatula-shaped dark-green leaves; very brilliant burnt-orange bloom.

Stelis cilaris. Tongue-shaped dark-green leaves; tiny red blooms.

S. micrantha. Six-inch green foliage; tiny greenish-white flowers.

Philodendrons

The 250 species of philodendrons (native to the tropical parts of America) offer many different leaf shapes: small, medium, large; heart and oval; some with serrated edges and others with scalloped leaves, solid or cutleaf. Some are climbing plants, others self-heading, bearing leaves in a central crown. In nature, philodendrons grow in shady wet forests and jungles. The jungle is warm during the day but it cools in the evening. In our homes, daytime temperatures are warm too, but at night, homes generally cool down, so they afford good conditions for philodendrons.

Philodendrons grow best in a porous soil: ⅓ sand, ⅓ peat moss, and ⅓ rich loam. Don't flood the plants, but try to keep the soil evenly moist all year. Feed moderately every other month through the year. Mature vining philodendrons have the habit of producing smaller leaves than the base leaves after a time. In most cases this is because the nutrients in the soil are exhausted; repot the plants with fresh soil. (Most philodendrons will also grow just as well in clear water, occasionally changed, as if potted in soil.) Wipe leaves occasionally with a damp cloth to keep them shiny. Place plants 4 to 6 inches from lamps; a two-lamp setup is okay. Here are some of the smaller philodendrons (none over 30 inches):

>   *P. andreanum*. Handsome arrow-shaped foliage; needs moisture and warmth. Grows large.
>   *P. cordatum* (*P. oxycardium*). The heart-leaf plant. Glossy green leaves. Grows in water or soil.
>   *P. hastatum variegatum*. New. Yellow-and-green leaves.
>   *P. panduraeforme*. Scalloped olive-green leaves; grows low.
>   *P. pertusum*. A tough, robust grower with deep-lobed heart-shaped leaves. Variegated form of yellow and green also available.
>   *P. soderoi*. Large or small forms with mottled leaves, red stems.
>   *P. squamiferum*. Unusual leaf design; good accent plant.
>   *P. verrucosum*. Outstanding. Exotic satin-sheen foliage. Needs warmth and humidity.
>   *P. wendlandii*. Self-heading cabbage type. Dense rosettes of waxy green tongue-shaped leaves; grows large.

62

5·Accent Plants Under Incandescent Light

UNDER INCANDESCENT or mercury vapor light, room plants, that is, those used as decorative elements, are in somewhat different conditions than shelf-garden plants; they are not necessarily in a confined area nor are they always grouped with other plants. Accent plants *must* have adequate humidity. This can be accomplished in several ways that will be discussed later in the chapter. Potting a large plant is different from potting a small one. Also, the planting technique for potting a large plant is different from that used in potting a small one. And because ceiling tracks with appropriate fixtures and lamps are used for accent plants, how to select hardware to harmonize with the room is a further consideration, as is the container for the plant—this, too, must be appropriate for the plant and the room.

SPECIMEN PLANTS

A plant that is mature, large, and at its peak form is called a specimen or decorator plant. It can be 8 or 12 feet tall, a tree or a shrub, a succulent or a bromeliad. It can be massive and branching or delicate and fragile in appearance. Its form may be columnar, pyramidal, or globelike, and there are all kinds of plants for all kinds of situations. A specimen plant can cost as much as a piece of furniture, but if properly cared for it will last for many years. Often all that is needed as a room feature is one striking specimen plant under two overhead lighting fixtures or a group of plants along a window wall (supplemental incandescent light can be mounted in ceilings). Your choice of a plant should be dictated by the furnishings, size, shape, and character of the room, the color and texture of a plant's leaves and its resistance to insects and disease.

Once it was difficult to locate large plants and impossible to have them shipped so that they would arrive in good condition. Now several suppliers in large cities (for example, The Greenhouse in New York and Chicago) stock decorator plants that can be purchased or rented on a monthly basis. Mail-order suppliers and local retail nurseries also stock specimen plants, and air freight carries plants overnight from almost any place in the United States. Just last week I received some 8-foot orchids in perfect condition; the plants arrived in California sixteen hours after leaving Chicago.

There are many plants that will thrive indefinitely indoors with artificial light, but some do better than others. The ficus family has many species with graceful branches and finely toothed leaves. Use two 150-watt, incandescent, wide floodlights to illuminate and keep these plants healthy and make them a dramatic addition to any room. Large succulents and cacti will thrive with one 150-watt incandescent floodlight.

To determine the position of a plant in a room, draw a rough sketch (detailed drawings are not necessary). Put in the furniture and accessories; merely use shapes and forms: round, square, rectangular, and so forth. Once the plan is drawn, sketch in plants where you think you'll want them. Pay attention to vertical and horizontal accents, and make small arrow signs that indicate the location of light fixtures and the direction of the light beam. If the first arrangement is not pleasing, do another until an attractive total picture is created. Specimen plants are not easy to move around once potted, though you may wish to experiment with positioning when the plant is brought in on a dolly (see page 67).

The following specimen plants have been chosen because they grow well indoors and have some outstanding characteristics. The plants can be grown with a pair of 150-watt incandescent floodlamps at a distance of 36 inches and at a 30° angle. Or you can use mercury vapor lamps at greater distances.

Decorator (Specimen) Plants

Agave americana variegata. Century plant. Broad lance-shaped leaves; bold design. Easy to grow; needs large container. Can grow to 5 inches in diameter.

Araucaria excelsa. Norfolk pine. Can grow to 7 feet; looks like a Christmas tree.

Chamaedorea erumpens. Bamboo palm. A large 48- to 60-inch palm that looks like a fern. An absolutely spectacular room plant.

Dieffenbachia bowmannii. Chartreuse foliage. Grows to 36 inches.

D. hoffmanni. Showy white leaf pattern. To 48 inches.

D. oerstedii variegata. Dark green leaf with white midrib. To 40 inches.

D. picta 'Rudolph Roehrs'. Arching leaves in shades of green. To 48 inches.

D. splendens. Velvety green foliage with white dots. To 48 inches.

Dizygotheca elegantissima. Spider aralia. Dark-green scalloped leaves edged in red in frond growth; tall, reedlike stems. To 60 inches.

Dracaena fragrans massangeana. Corn plant. Cream-colored stripes on broad deep green leaves. Grows somewhat like a palm from a central core and becomes a handsome 6-foot tree in a few years.

D. godseffiana. Green leaves spattered with yellow; bushy growth, small size. To 30 inches.

D. marginata. Well known and very expensive. Branching plant with compounds of sword-shaped leaves. To 6 feet.

D. sanderiana. Gray-green white-margined foliage. To 40 inches.

Ferns. Large group with many medium-sized appealing plants. Includes species of Adiantum, Asplenium, Davallia, and Nephrolepis. Many sizes; generally 36 inches in diameter.

Ficus benjamina. To 8 feet; small, lacy, delicate leaves.

F. elastica decora. Oval, glossy green leaves with ivory veins. To 60 inches.

F. retusa. Another good ficus. To 8 feet.

Howea forsteriana. Sentry palm. Graceful fronds with slender stalks. Slow-growing; does well indoors. To 60 inches.

Pandandus veitchii. Corkscrew pine. A spiral arrangement of long glossy green leaves. Handsome, amenable plant. To 48 inches.

Philodendron bipinnatifidum. Large, deeply lobed leaves on arching stems. Always handsome. To 48 inches.

P. monstera deliciosa. Swiss cheese plant. Big and bold, with massive leaves. To 72 inches.

P. wendlandii. Broad, dark-green leaves in a compact rosette. To 40 inches in diameter.

Pittosporum tobira variegata. Tongue-shaped, rich green leaves edged in white. Compact growth to 40 inches.

Podocarpus macrophylla maki. Rich, green, tufted-type leaves in compact growth. To 30 inches.

Raphis excelsa. A handsome palm, with dark-green, almost brittle leaves on tall stems. Grows dense and massive with good care. To 30 inches.

Schefflera acontifolia. Umbrella tree. A tall, branching plant with leaflets that form small canopies. Hardy and tolerant of indoor conditions. Can grow into small tree. To 8 feet.

Yucca aloifolia. Spanish dagger. Pointed erect leaves make this a dramatic plant for room decor. Robust and strong and can live for a dozen years. Grows to 48 inches.

CONTAINERS AND CARE

Specimen plants will need a 20- to 28-inch container. Choose one that is in character with the plant. Generally, bushy plants like pittosporum or podocarpus look best in tubs. Sculptural branching plants such as *Dracaena marginata* and citrus are most effective in wooden boxes and tubs, and large palms look best in Spanish pots. Lacy plants like bamboos and *Ficus ben-*

Incandescent lamps are used in a panel over a lovely Raphis excelsa *to keep it in good health. (Photo by Max Eckert)*

jamina are ideal in ornate containers—jardinieres or urns.

A 20-inch container filled with soil weighs about 250 pounds, so it is almost impossible to move, once it is in place. Buy dollies (sold at nurseries) to put under containers so you can move plants around if necessary.

Use the best possible soil for large plants. Soil should be porous in texture to allow excess water to drain freely. You can buy soil in sacks or in bulk. For my specimen plants under incandescent light I use 1 part garden loam, 1 part leaf mold, and 1 part sand. Avoid "soilless" mixes. These are composed of sphagnum peat moss and perlite or vermiculite; sufficient nutrients must be added to them on a regular schedule for good plant growth, and this becomes quite a chore.

Water specimen plants heavily and deeply and then allow them to dry out before watering them again. Once every few months move them to an area where you can leach the soil—that is, soak

67

plants in a large tub or keep water flowing into the soil for 5 or 10 minutes to drain away acids and salts that build up in the soil and can harm roots.

Feed plants with a general plant food (10–10–5) twice a month through spring and summer, once a month in fall, and not at all in winter.

Average room temperatures suit most accent plants, but mist foliage occasionally with a sprayer to furnish additional humidity. Make sure plants have good air circulation but are out of drafts and away from hot-air registers. Never place an accent plant near an outside door because the opening and closing of the door will create cold blasts of air that are harmful to plants in winter.

DISPLAY-LIGHTING MECHANICS

A few years ago, lighting large indoor plants was difficult because there were few attractive fixtures or simple methods of installing them. Generally, the accommodations for the fixture had to be made at the time the house was under construction and before furnishings or plants had been chosen. Furthermore, most fixtures were of institutional design, hardly pleasing in the house.

Usually the basic fixture of display lighting was a single bullet- or cone-shaped unit mounted on a wall or ceiling or an eye-ball swivel-type unit recessed in the ceiling. Either design was hardly attractive and required special installation.

Today, the lighting industry has made great advances in display lighting designs that are easy to install and flexible in a wide variety of indoor situations. This new lighting technique is called a track system.

Fluorescent lamps in square panels and incandescent pin spots are used to provide light for this attractive plant display. (Photo courtesy General Electric Co.)

TRACK-SYSTEM LIGHTING

The track for the fixtures is a strip of hardware mounted on a ceiling or wall. Contemporary fixtures can be attached to the track at any given point and can be angled in almost any direction. If you have a large indoor plant in a corner without a light above it, simply buy another fixture and attach it to the channel (and you *can* do it yourself), thus adjusting the light to the plant rather than moving the plant to the light, which is not often practical.

Another advantage of track lighting is that it doesn't have to be installed before the house is completed; it is easy to put it in after construction without undue cost to the homeowner. However, it is best to have an electrician install the system. My installation fee for a 4-foot track with four lamps was $90 plus the cost of track and lamps.

This movable display-lighting system (called Power Trac by the Halo Lighting Company and Lite Span by Lightolier Company) can be used in straight lines or in an infinite variety of patterns to cover almost any desired plant area. The hardware is sleek and blends well with almost any indoor setting; it is to be seen as well as used.

One of the two floodlamps keeps this mammoth schefflera in robust health; skylight in ceiling also provides natural light for the plants. (Photo by Max Eckert)

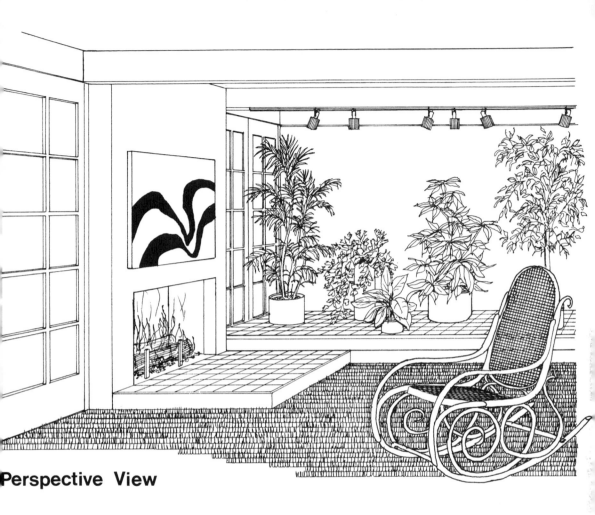

Perspective View

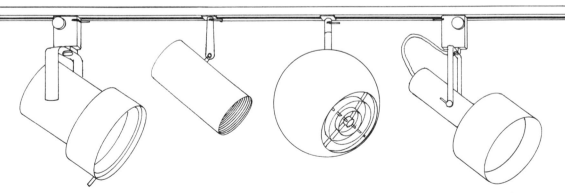

Plants with Accent Lights

Indoor garden of foliage plants is maintained with five floodlamps. (Photo courtesy General Electric Co.)

Lamps

A floodlight is the lamp most suitable for display lighting of plants. Whereas a spotlight strikes only one area of a plant, a floodlight illuminates almost the entire plant, depending on its size. And with floodlights there is no sharply defined beam pattern; the most intense light is at the outer limits, with the illumination dropping to 10 percent of the maximum at the center of the cone.

The heat radiated from incandescent lamps can, if too close, burn foliage, so for safety place lamps 3 feet from the plant and generally use a 200-watt bulb. If more light is needed (300 or 500 watts), use heat-absorbing lenses that snap onto fixtures. These lenses filter out 80 percent of the heat, so lamps can be placed closer to the subject if necessary, and higher wattages can be used without any danger. Mercury vapor lamps can also be used for greater light intensity.

Fixtures

There are numerous lighting fixtures for display use. Most are of a can-type design: the lamp is recessed in a metal cylinder that directs the light downward in an arc. These fixtures come in brushed aluminum with black trim or in white semigloss enamel. Most fixtures are designed specifically for use with reflector or

72

Perspective View

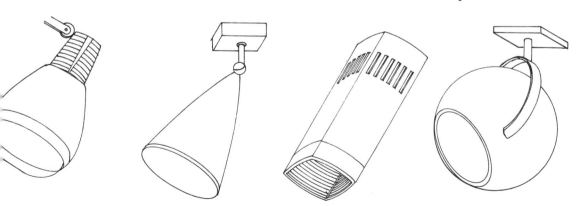

Corner Plant Group—Mercury Vapor Lights

73

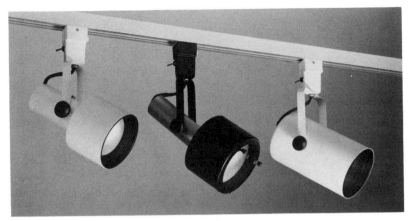

Fixtures for floodlamps come in many designs and colors. (Photo by Halo Lighting Co.)

projector lamps. However, special fixtures for the General Electric Cool-Beam lamp and low-voltage lamps are available. The housings are designed to provide complete directional adjustment, both horizontal and vertical; knurled bakelite knobs lock the vertical positioning. All finishes are baked to guarantee durability.

The fixtures attach to the track with a unique adapter connector: simply twist the fixture to lock it into position and to provide a polarized electrical connection. Several fixtures also have adapter hardware for heat-reducing glass lenses.

There are hundreds of fixture designs and sizes, and what you use depends on your budget and taste.

Closeup of incandescent lamp fixture. Fixture can be swiveled in two directions. (Photo by Prescolite Co.)

6·Propagation

EVERYONE LIKES SOMETHING for nothing, and under lights plants are generous with offspring. Propagating plants under natural light is sometimes difficult, but with controlled light seeds sprout easily and cuttings root readily without fuss or bother. When I start seedlings or cuttings under lights I know they will grow; this is not always true with propagation under natural light. And recent reports from many periodicals indicate that plants started under lights are superior to those grown in greenhouses.

PROPAGATING CASES AND MEDIUMS

Any container that has a cover—casserole, baking dish, hatbox—makes a good growing case for seeds. So do the small commercial greenhouses with plastic hoods and electric cables for bottom heat to insure seed germination. Some of these greenhouses have their own fluorescent fixtures; all come with planting trays, and some with wick-fed automatic watering devices. You can also use commercial bedding plant bins (available from suppliers) for starting plants. The top section is properly drained, and the bottom part is waterproof to catch runoff water. Put stakes (small sticks) in the growing medium and cover with

Many different kinds of containers can be used for starting seeds under lights. Household items as well as standard clay pots do fine. (Photo by Jack Barnick)

plastic to make a miniature tent to use as a propagating case and to provide humidity.

There are dozens of mixes for growing seeds: milled sphagnum, vermiculite, sand, peat moss, and so forth. Use the material that gives you the best results after some experimentation. I prefer vermiculite; it is available in packages at most supermarkets and florists, is easy to work with, and is sterile (weed and disease organisms are eliminated). Sand and peat moss have to be sterilized.

SEEDS AND CUTTINGS

For germinating seeds and rooting cuttings use 10 lamp watts per square foot of growing area; my setup for seedlings is four 40-watt, 48-inch warm fluorescent lamps. Cover the seeds only very lightly with the propagating mix and then comb or scrape the surface somewhat after soaking the medium to allow better penetration of light, and to permit oxygen to enter the seeds. For seed germination keep the temperature about 10°

Here, seeds are placed in sphagnum in mayonnaise jar, which provides good humidity. Later they will be placed under fluorescent lamps. (Photo by Jack Barnick)

higher than for normal daytime growing. A heating cable sold at suppliers is often recommended to help keep the temperature high, but I have never had to use one—most of my seeds have germinated without it.

Sturdy seedlings are produced when the amount of red exceeds the far red light. With higher levels of red the seedlings tend to be greener and shorter, with well-developed leaves and stems. For early seedlings, fluorescent lamps should be used, because incandescent lamps have a high level of far red radiation, which opposes the effects of red light, and is not desirable for seedlings.

If you are propagating only a few seeds in a small pot, slip a plastic bag over it to ensure a humid atmosphere. Keep the growing mix evenly moist. The time it takes for seeds to sprout depends on the type of plant you are growing.

Don't cover begonia seeds and many other seeds that are so fine they are like powder. Sow them as thinly as possible on the vermiculite. (Mixing the seeds with sand makes the distribution easier.) Cover larger seeds like coleus and impatiens only very slightly, to one third their depth.

When germination shows, move the seedlings closer to the lamps. And as soon as they are large enough to handle, transplant seedlings to individual or community pots containing standard soil—the sooner the better.

Stem Cuttings

For stem cuttings, select sturdy shoots, usually in spring. Take off 4-inch pieces, cutting them just below a leaf node (the little swelling on the stem), and remove the foliage from the lower 2 inches. I keep a jar of water with a few granules of charcoal on the window sill, and often I just pop in cuttings of wax begonias or African violets and set them under lights; sometimes I put a plastic bag over the jar to increase humidity. Some plants can be propagated this way, but the majority, like tradescantia and coleus, generally need the warmth and protection of a case.

Leaf Cuttings

With leaf cuttings—rex begonias, kalanchoes, and others— cut across the leaf veins in several places on the underside; I use a razor blade. Place the leaves right side up, flat on the sand in a propagating case, with the stems in the sand, about 6 to 8 inches from the lamps. To ensure contact between the leaf and the medium, weight the leaf with pebbles. Plantlets soon appear along the cuts and draw nourishment from the old leaf. When the new plants can be handled easily, cut them from the parent leaf and pot them separately. Give them more light now; place them 4 to 6 inches from the lamps. Leaf cuttings taken in spring or summer are more apt to produce plants than those taken in fall or winter.

78

Air Layering

When the rubber tree or the philodendron in the living room gets too big, take advantage of your light setups to start new plants by air layering. This sounds difficult, and people are reluctant to try it, but it is an easy way to get new plants to grow under lights until they are big enough for living-room decoration.

Peel off the bark (about 1 or 2 inches) of the plant below a leaf joint. Scrape away the ring of outer tissue. Then wrap a big clump of moist moss around the bare wood and cover it with a piece of plastic secured at top and bottom with string; there must be a moistureproof seal for root growth to start. When the moss is filled with roots, cut off the new plant below the root ball, and put the fledgling in a very porous mix. Place under lights. In a few more months, pot the plant for permanent placement in the light garden. The mother plant will continue growing.

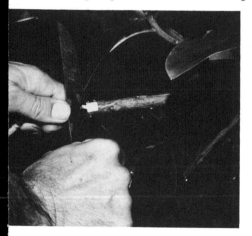

Making cut for air layering. (Photo by Jack Barnick)

Sphagnum being wrapped around girdled cut. (Photo by U.S. Department of Agriculture)

Air layer wrapped in plastic and tied at ends. (Photo by U.S. Department of Agriculture)

The offset on this palm is ready to be separately potted, then placed under lights for future growth. (Photo by Matthew Barr)

Stolons and Offsets

Plants like chlorophytum, episcia, and neomarica produce stolons, or runners. Take them about 3 inches long, and handle them like cuttings. Roots develop and plants are ready for fresh soil in about 4 weeks to 4 months, depending on the type.

Bromeliads, some orchids, gesneriads, and agaves develop suckers or offsets at the base of the mature plant. When they are 2 to 4 inches long, cut them off with a sterile knife and root them as you do cuttings.

Division

Plants that have trunks or multiple crowns, for example, some orchids, clivia, spathiphyllum, and several ferns, can be reproduced by division. Pull a plant apart so that each section has a bit of crown and some roots. If plants are massive or woody, sever the growth with a clean, sharp knife. Cut off the foliage to encourage new growth; plant the divisions in small pots of porous soil and put them under lights, 6 to 8 inches from the lamps.

Runners like these from chlorophytum can be cut and placed in growing medium for artificial light growing. (Photo by Merry Gardens)

Shrub and Tree Cuttings

You can also take cuttings of fruit trees or of shrubs (abutilon, aralia, azalea, gardenia) by severing about 4 inches of the stem having at least two leaf nodes. Remove the leaves, dip cut edge of stem lightly in hormone powder, and insert the cuttings carefully so the powder doesn't come off in the medium. Place 6 to 8 inches from the lamps. When plants are rooted, put them in pots of rich soil, or try them in the outdoor garden.

81

7·Pests and Diseases

CATCHING TROUBLE before it starts is the key to pestfree indoor gardening—once insects and disease have a foothold they are difficult to get rid of. To avoid problems follow these suggestions:

1. Always isolate new plants for about a week so that if there are any insects they can be detected. As an added precaution against harboring insects, spray each new plant with plain water from the kitchen sink immediately upon bringing it home.
2. Soak plants to the pot rim in a sinkful of water to eliminate unwanted guests in the soil.
3. Keep plants well groomed; pick off dead leaves and faded flowers.
4. Wipe or mist foliage, being sure to include the undersides of leaves, with tepid water at least once a week. This cleansing removes insect eggs and spider mites and in general discourages other pests.
5. Once a month, pick up each pot and carefully inspect the plant from above and below for possible insects. (With very heavy tubs that cannot be moved, inspect leaves frequently right where they are.)
6. Use a stiff brush to remove algae that may have accumulated on the pot surfaces.

7. Occasionally scan leaves—both top surface and underside—with a magnifying glass to help you spot thrips, white flies, and red spiders, insects that are difficult to see with the naked eye.

HOME REMEDIES

There is little sense in using poisonous sprays in the home unless a plant is so severely attacked that nothing else will save it. Use home remedies before resorting to pesticides. If you discover a few insects, try to eliminate them with a vigorous spray of soapy water followed by a rinse in tepid water. A mixture of soap and water often deters red spiders; follow with a cleansing rinse. Eradicate mealybugs with a solution of equal parts alcohol and water followed by a washing with soap and water and a rinse of clear water. Repeat the application twice a week for 3 weeks. Persistence is necessary. Pour hot water (90° F.) over soil to chase springtails into the saucer; then wash them away.

INSECTICIDES

If an infestation is severe and you must use insecticides, buy organic ones such as Rotenone and Pyrethrum. But first determine what insect you are fighting. A miticide will not cure disease, and the spray that kills mealybugs will not deter scale. Know what you are fighting before you start battle. When you are using pesticides, mix them carefully according to the directions on the package and take note of precautions. Spray plants, or make a pail of solution and dunk the foliage in it for a few minutes. Be sure to cover the soil with a piece of aluminum foil, and don't put the ailing plant immediately back under lights; let it dry, out of the sun, and then rinse it with clear water.

If you don't want to mix solutions, buy an all-purpose aerosol

83

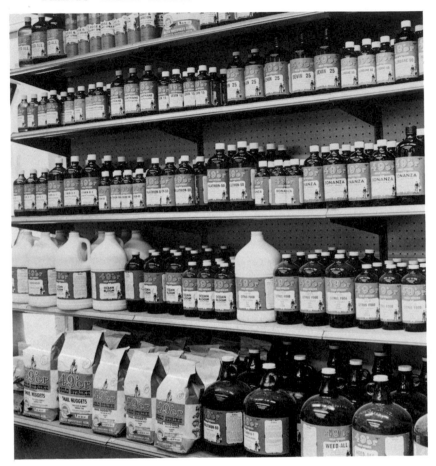

Nurseries stock an array of insecticides. It is best to use them only when absolutely necessary, and then with extreme caution. (Photo by Matthew Barr)

preventative. These pushbutton cans are expensive, but they are convenient. Spray the whole plant—stems, leaves—under as well as over the foliage. Don't spray at close range; the recommended distance is 12 to 14 inches from the plant.

Systemics (insecticides applied to the soil) are another convenience in the battle of the bugs, but most of the systemics are very poisonous, so use them with extreme caution and keep treated plants away from pets or children. Systemics protect plants from sucking and chewing insects from 6 to 8 weeks. One application is all that is necessary; spread the granules over the soil and water thoroughly. The roots of the plant draw the insecticide into the sap stream and make it toxic to insects. There are several systemics sold at nurseries under various trade names: Cygon 2E, Scope, and others.

Some plants attract more insects than others; some are impervious to attack. Bromeliads and orchids, with their stiff succulent leaves, are rarely bothered by pests except scale. Unfortunately the popular African violet is host to many insects, cyclamen mite being the most bothersome. Mealybugs seem to have little preference and are found on all kinds of plants; red spider mites are very partial to impatiens and gardenias and can be fatal if not recognized in an early stage. Scale quite often selects citrus for a meal, and aphids enjoy a variety in their diet, feasting on gesneriads, begonias, or any plant at hand. Yet most of these insects can be easily eradicated if found early.

Nematodes, on the other hand, are fatal. These are microscopic eelworms that inhabit the roots (occasionally leaves too) of plants. Usually, plants stop growing, and you can see evidence of the attack when you remove the plant from its pot and examine the roots: swollen nodes appear along the roots. There is no "cure" for these insects; you must discard the plant.

VIRUS AND FUNGUS DISEASES

I don't try to cope with virus in orchids or fungus disease in plants. There are some good fungicides, but the scope of fungus disease is vast, and it is difficult to know what you're fighting. Fungus and bacterial diseases of foliage are rarely found on house plants. A combination of darkness and wet foilage is an invitation for these diseases, but under lights there is little possibility of plants contracting them.

85

PEST AND REMEDY CHART FOR ALL PLANTS

What to Look For	Cause	Remedy
White cottony clusters in stem and leaf axils	Mealybugs	Alcohol on Q-tips; for severe infestations use Diazinon
Leaves deformed, streaked, or silvery with dark specks	Thrips	Pyrethrum
Green, black, red, or pink insects on new growth; sticky, shiny leaves	Aphids	Rotenone
Plants stunted, crowns bunched, leaves cupped up or down	Cyclamen or broad mite	Systemics
Fine webs at leaf and stem axils; leaves mottled, turning gray or brown	Red spider mites	Spray with water frequently; also, use soap-and-water solution
Swarming insects that leave sooty deposits; leaves stippled or yellow	White fly	Rotenone
Clusters of brown, black, or gray hard-shelled insects	Scale	Diazinon
Holes in leaves	Slugs or snails	Snare-all
Gray, watery green, or yellow leaves	Bacterial blight	Zineb
Flowers, leaves, and stalks spotted or circled	Virus	Discard plant

86

Appendixes

1 · Where to Buy Plants

THERE ARE HUNDREDS of mail-order companies that sell plants; some specialize in geraniums, others in orchids or bromeliads. There are companies that supply seeds and bulbs, and many companies have assortments of house plants.

Almost all suppliers furnish price lists or catalogs; some are free, others carry a nominal charge. Do order these catalogs; they contain a wealth of information. All the mail-order houses welcome personal visits.

All kinds of plants can be shipped, and suppliers furnish excellent packing and crating. I don't recommend having plants shipped during very hot or very cold weather, but other people tell me they have received shipments in winter and summer without harm to the plants.

I have personally known and/or used and found to be reliable the following suppliers (C = catalog, L = list):

Alberts & Merkel Bros.　　　　　Orchids, bromeliads. C.
Boynton Beach, Fla. 33435

Beahm Gardens　　　　　　　　Succulents and cacti. C.
2686 Paloma St.
Pasadena, Calif. 91107

Buell's Greenhouses　　　　　　Gloxinias and African violets. C.
Eastford, Conn. 06242

Burgess Seed & Plant Co. Galesburg, Mich. 49053	House plants. C.
W. Atlee Burpee Co. Philadelphia, Pa. 19132	Seeds and bulbs. C.
Fischer Greenhouses Linwood, New Jersey 08221	African violets and other gesneriads. C.
Hausermann's Orchids Box 363 Elmhurst, Ill. 60128	Wide variety of orchids. C.
Henrietta's Nursery 1345 N. Brawley Fresno, Calif. 93705	Good selection of cacti and succulents. C.
Margaret Ilgenfritz Monroe, Michigan 48161	All kinds of orchids. C and L.
Michael J. Kartuz 92 Chestnut Street Wilmington, Mass. 01887	House plants. L.
Rod McLellan Co. 1450 El Camino Real South San Franciso, Calif. 94080	Orchids. C.
Merry Gardens Camden, Me. 04843	Good selection of house plants. C.
George W. Park Seed Co. Greenwood, S.C. 29647	House plants, seeds, and bulbs. C.
Tinari Greenhouses Bethayres, Pa. 19006	African violets and other gesneriads. C.
Wilson Bros. Roachdale, Ind. 46172	Geraniums and other house plants. C.

2 · Where to Buy Lighting Equipment and Supplies

Floralite Co.
4124 East Oakwood Road
Oak Creek, Wisc. 53154

Fluorescent light equipment;
free folder.

House Plant Corner
P. O. Box 810
Oxford, Md. 21654

Supplies, equipment. Catalog 20
cents.

Lifelite
Radiant Color Co.
2800 Radiant Ave.
Richmond, Calif. 94804

Colorant sheets (plastic sheets to
screen out ultra-violet rays).
Free brochure.

Lord & Burnham
Irvington, N.Y. 10533

Fluorescent light units. Free
catalog.

George W. Park Seed Co.
Greenwood, S.C. 29647

Fluorescent light equipment. Free
catalog.

Harvey J. Ridge
1126 Arthur St.
Wausau, Wisc. 54401

Fluorescent light equipment. Free
list.

Shoplite Co.
650 Franklin Ave.
Nutley, N.J. 07110

Fluorescent light equipment; kits
and parts. Catalog 10 cents.

Tube Craft Inc.
1311 W. 80th St.
Cleveland, Ohio 44102

Floracarts, timers, and plant
trays. Free catalog.

3 · Pamphlets and Booklets on Lighting

Agricultural Research Service United States Department of Agriculture Beltsville, Md. 20705	Light and plant growth bulletins.
Duro-Test Corp. North Bergen, N.J. 07047	Technical data on lighting.
Edison Electric Institute 750 Third Ave. New York, N.Y. 10017	Free "Electric Gardening" pamphlet.
General Electric Co. Lamp Division Nela Park Cleveland, Ohio 44112	Light and plant growth bulletins.
Sylvania Electric Products, Inc. Sylvania Lighting Center Danvers, Mass. 01923	Bulletins and brochures.
Union Electric Co. St. Louis, Mo. 63166	Free color brochure, "Growing Plants Under Fluorescent Light."
Westinghouse Electric Corp. Lamp Division Bloomfield, N.J. 07003	Technical and research bulletins.

4 · Plant Societies and Their Publications

African Violet Society of America
P. O. Box 1326
Knoxville, Tenn. 37901

African Violet Magazine

American Begonia Society
1510 Kimberly Avenue
Anaheim, Calif. 92802

The Begonian

American Gesneria Society and
    Saintpaulia International
    Indoor Gardener Publishing Co.
1800 Grand Avenue
Knoxville, Tenn. 37901

Gesneria Saintpaulia News

American Gloxinia Society
Eastford, Conn.

The Gloxinian

American Orchid Society
Botanical Museum of Harvard
    University
Cambridge, Mass. 02138

*American Orchid Society
Bulletin*

Epiphyllum Society of America
4400 Portola Avenue
Los Angeles, Calif. 90026

Bulletin

Indoor Light Gardening Society
    of America, Inc.
Mrs. Fred D. Peden
4 Wildwood Rd.
Greensville, S. C. 29607

The News

5 · Reading for Artificial Light Gardeners

Artificial Light and Horticulture, C. W. Canham, Centrex Publishing Company, Eindhoven, Holland, 1968.

Begonias, Indoors and Out, Jack Kramer, E. P. Dutton and Company, Inc., New York, 1967.

Cacti and Other Succulents, Claude Chidamian, Doubleday and Company, Inc., Garden City, New York, 1958.

Fluorescent Light Gardening, E. C. Cherry, Van Nostrand Reinhold Company, New York, 1965.

Gardening Indoors Under Lights, F. H. and J. L. Kranz, The Viking Press, Inc., New York, 1957.

Gardening Under Lights, Elvin McDonald, Doubleday and Company, Inc., Garden City, New York, 1966.

Gesneriads and How to Grow Them, Peggy Schulz (ed.), Diversity Books, Kansas City, Mo., 1967.

Growing Orchids at Your Windows, Jack Kramer, Hawthorn Books, Inc., 1973.

Growing Plants Under Artificial Light, Peggy Schulz, M. Barrows and Company, Inc., New York, 1955.

94

APPENDIXES

Light and Plant Growth, R. Van Der Veen and G. Meijer, Eindhoven, Holland—Phillips Technical Library, 1959, distributed by Macmillan, New York.

The Orchids, Carl L. Withner, The Ronald Press Company, New York, 1961.

MU8D